We Used to Dream of Freedom is a _____ , ____ account of a life lived outside convention yet guided by the most important human values: freedom, family, compassion, memory, and self-knowledge. Frank, touching, thoughtful, and surprising, Chaiton's memoir is a testament to the healing and understanding, and ultimately, love that is possible when a family shares the difficult stories, and speaks the unspeakable.

— GARY BARWIN, author of *Yiddish for Pirates*

We children of Holocaust survivors live precariously, with so much trauma ingrained in us, and so many reasons to somehow break free and strive for success. While my survivor parents were adamant about telling their war stories incessantly, many others, like Sam Chaiton's parents, insisted on keeping their stories a secret. *We Used to Dream of Freedom* paints a poignant portrait of the devastating damage mystery and dark secrets can do to family ties. Chaiton's fearless and moving memoir is a precious gift to anyone who yearns for a better understanding of intergenerational trauma and the path to true liberation.

— JEANNE BEKER, author, fashion editor, and television personality

A bold, honest, and absorbing exploration of how the Holocaust and its secrets continue to traumatize a second generation. Chaiton's flight from familial dysfunction sets him on an extraordinary path, leading to the freedom of Rubin "Hurricane" Carter. The author's stunning realization then brings us full circle: the trajectory of his Jewish survivor parents and the African American boxer "are scarily similar in the injustices of their incarcerations, based entirely on racism rather than reason." A timely and gripping read.

— LISA BRAHIN, author of *Tears Over Russia*

A powerful "second generation" memoir that captures the impact of growing up in a family with two survivor parents who imposed total silence about their Holocaust experiences. Among the five sons, Sam's response was decades of alienation and disappearance but ultimately healing and reconciliation after uncovering his parents' horrific stories.

— CHRISTOPHER R. BROWNING, professor emeritus of history, University of North Carolina at Chapel Hill

This multi-faceted memoir is the story of Chaiton's years raised in a Holocaust survivor family and followed by his unique adventurous journey working through trauma, reinvention, and understanding. In our current world of daunting change and challenge, his story will resonate with all ages, cultures, and nationalities who are struggling to maintain their equilibrium.

— PAULA DAVID, MSW, Ph.D., survivor trauma expert

You will be transported through time and memory by Sam Chaiton's stunning memoir. With remarkable honesty, clarity, and evocative prose, Chaiton shares a storied life touching on family, art, activism, the Holocaust, and his relationship and role in the exoneration of Rubin "Hurricane" Carter. *We Used to Dream of Freedom* is a must read.

— ALAN DILWORTH, artistic director, Necessary Angel Theatre Company

It is as if the wisdom of Søren Kierkegaard — "life can only be understood backwards, but it must be lived forwards" — set in motion Sam Chaiton's memoir, as a guiding directive through a profound journey of self-discovery and soulful reclamation of his parents' past.

— BERNICE EISENSTEIN, author of *I Was a Child of Holocaust Survivors*

Sam Chaiton's *We Used to Dream of Freedom* is a brilliant read, abounding with clear-eyed humanity, telling us about an extraordinary life in which Chaiton resets the scales of justice, not just for himself and his family but for all of us.

— JAMES LOCKYER, co-founder, Innocence Canada

Sam dances through his life-affirming meeting with the early modern dance movement at a time we know little about in writing; communal living à la "summer of love"; a persistent urge to right wrongs in himself and in the world at large. He finds his family through leaving them behind — his siblings for two decades, his parents forever — but a solid nuclear circle of dependable friends surround him and care for him. I found the book extremely relatable as a Canadian-born dance artist with roots in Europe through my own father's parents, themselves saved by ingenuity, and silence, from the horrors of WWII.

—JAMES KUDELKA, choreographer

From his beginnings as a child of Holocaust survivors (like me) dreaming of a life in the arts (also like me!), through his eventual role in helping to secure Rubin "Hurricane" Carter's freedom, and beyond, comes Sam Chaiton's frank, wholly engaging memoir. I did not know him until the journey he took into his family's heart-rending history led him from Wierzbnik, Poland, to Toronto, Canada, — and right to my door. The synchronicity of our two families' experiences during WWII is astounding. The slave number that the Nazis forcibly tattooed on my mother, Manya's, arm in Auschwitz is a mere fifteen numbers apart from the one Sam's mother, Luba, bore since that terrifying first day of their incarceration. They were in the very same lineup, and that was just one coincidence on their tortured road to freedom. What a trip.

— GEDDY LEE, musician, Rush

Sam Chaiton's search for familial love and connection drew him into a life marked by keen curiosity, cycles of experimentation, risk, accomplishment, success, loss, acts of compassion, and eventually to the revelation of his family's buried past. May our obstacles goad us to live lives that make a difference, as Sam's has.

— DENISE FUJIWARA, artistic director,
Fujiwara Dance Inventions

A vividly written, dramatic personal memoir of activism, artistry, alienation, and ultimately, affirmation, depicting a life lived in the murky after-shadows of the Holocaust.

— GABOR MATÉ, M.D., author of *The Myth of Normal*

Given his experiences as a child of Holocaust survivors, I understand why Sam dedicated his life to righting wrongs and fighting for justice for the innocent, including Rubin "Hurricane" Carter and me.

— GUY PAUL MORIN

No two Holocaust survivors' stories are alike. Each is unique unto itself. And as Sam Chaiton's revealing, artfully written, and timely autobiography, *We Used to Dream of Freedom*, makes clear, this is equally true for survivors' children raised in the shadow of the Holocaust. Chaiton's second-generation story, singularly his own, is a conversation starter that deserves to be read.

— HAROLD TROPER, Canadian historian
and co-author of *None Is Too Many*

WE USED TO DREAM OF FREEDOM

We used to Dream of Freedom

A Memoir of Family, the Holocaust, and the Stories We Don't Tell

Sam Chaiton

DUNDURN
PRESS

Publisher: Meghan Macdonald | Acquiring editors: Julia Kim & Kwame Scott Fraser | Editor: Julia Kim
Cover designer: Laura Boyle
Cover image: deer: unsplash/_joanne_; dancer: unsplash/Karsten Winegeart; family photo provided by the author

Library and Archives Canada Cataloguing in Publication

Title: We used to dream of freedom : a memoir of family, the Holocaust, and the stories we don't tell / Sam Chaiton.
Names: Chaiton, Sam, 1950- author.
Description: Includes bibliographical references.
Identifiers: Canadiana (print) 20240349105 | Canadiana (ebook) 20240349121 | ISBN 9781459754683 (softcover) | ISBN 9781459754690 (PDF) | ISBN 9781459754706 (EPUB)
Subjects: LCSH: Chaiton, Sam, 1950- | LCSH: Children of Holocaust survivors—Canada—Biography. | LCSH: Holocaust survivors—Canada—Biography. | LCSH: Jews—Canada—Biography. | LCSH: Children of Holocaust survivors—Psychology. | LCSH: Holocaust survivors—Psychology. | LCSH: Children of Holocaust survivors—Family relationships. | LCGFT: Autobiographies.
Classification: LCC FC106.J5 C429 2024 | DDC 940.53/18092271—dc23

We acknowledge the support of the Canada Council for the Arts and the Ontario Arts Council for our publishing program. We also acknowledge the financial support of the Government of Ontario, through the Ontario Book Publishing Tax Credit and Ontario Creates, and the Government of Canada.

Printed and bound in Canada.

Dundurn Press
1382 Queen Street East
Toronto, Ontario, Canada M4L 1C9
dundurn.com, @dundurnpress

פֿאַר טאַטעמאַמען
וואָס האָבן מיר געגעבן דאָס לעבן
For my father and mother
who gave me life

8 May

It is over. Our liberation has come, but she wears a prosaic face. No one has died of joy. No one has gone mad with excitement. When we used to dream of freedom, we bathed her with our tears. We crowned her with the garlands of our smiles and dreams. Now that she is here, she looks like a beggar, and we have nothing to give her.

— Chava Rosenfarb, "Bergen-Belsen Diary, 1945"
(translated from the Yiddish by Goldie Morgentaler)

Contents

Prologue 1

1   Palmerston 7

2   Reading and Bleeding 19

3   Place Holders 33

4   Enchantments 49

5   Disenchantments 61

6   Meshuga 79

7   Higher Education 91

8   Abroad 105

9   Waving Free 117

10   Beneath the Diamond Sky 127

11   Take Me Disappearing 143

12   De Profundis 161

13	Freeing the Hurricane	177
14	Reappearing	191
15	The First Law of Thermodynamics	215
16	Wierzbnik	233
17	Buttonholing the Past	253
	Epilogue	269
	Acknowledgements	275
	Notes	279
	About the Author	283

Prologue

A TURNING POINT IN MY RELATIONSHIP WITH MY parents came twenty-five years after they died. It happened that my partner, Lindy Green, at the request of Toronto's Ashkenaz Festival, was about to mount an exhibition at the Al Green Gallery where she was director and curator. The showing, entitled *I Am from Here*, would consist entirely of paintings by Maciej Frankiewicz, a young Polish artist, a Christian who, Lindy explained, was obsessed with the obliterated Jewish community that had thrived in his town before the war. He painted scenes of the shtetl as he imagined it. He also voluntarily tended its neglected Jewish cemetery.

I asked Lindy the name of the town.

"Starachowice," she said, and I looked blankly back at her. "It used to be called Wierzbnik."

"Uh, you won't believe this, but I think that's where my parents were from."

A special preview evening at the gallery was planned for members of Toronto's Wierzbniker Society, to which, I then remembered, my parents had belonged.

"Then you should be there."

Rachmil and Luba were Polish Jews who, unlike three million others in Poland, had managed to survive the Holocaust. But they wouldn't talk about it. My mother, except in rare moments, acted as if it had never happened. My father, a tailor, said little beyond dubious anecdotes depicting himself as a wily POW à la *Hogan's Heroes*. My two older brothers were born in Germany after the war, in the Bergen-Belsen Displaced Persons Camp. We five boys — Abie, Charlie, Sam, David, Harvey — knew little else and probing proved futile. We were shut out of our parents' personal histories, though the secret lives they steadfastly refused to share with us were still vivid in them — evident in their number tattoos, in their sudden outbursts of violence both physical and psychological, and in their insular interactions with fellow concentration camp survivors who shared a common language and history, comrades who were closer to them than my brothers and I would ever be.

The unvoiced trauma of my parents' history weighed heavily. I had hoped to countervail or at least soften the war's aftermath by being an obedient son, but the task was Sisyphean and could not be done without the boulder flattening my authentic self. There was no space in their suffering for a child's independent existence, needs, inclinations, desires. Going against survivor parents was unthinkable. "This is what we survived for?" would be the inevitable response. I felt trapped and riven with guilt.

My siblings seemed more able to bear the burden. They were more compliant, if not content, with my parents' rigid demands on the shape our lives were to take. They would all become doctors and lawyers, the professionals my parents insisted we be. They would get married, have children, show up for Shabbos dinners every Friday night. Me, I fled.

I disappeared from my blood family for nearly two decades and created a new life for myself. I became part of a communal family of friends whose diverse personal histories were open books. We took to heart the ethos of the sixties' counterculture — questioning authority, valuing justice, fairness, equity, and brotherhood, not just as dreamers, but as doers. Together we helped free former American prizefighter Rubin "Hurricane" Carter from an extended nightmare of wrongful imprisonment in New Jersey. His triple murder conviction was overthrown and he was released the same year a car crash ended my mother's and father's lives.

I charily agreed to attend Lindy's art show but was beset with second thoughts. I had always hoped to discover more — anything — about my parents' old country history, yet the prospect terrified me. I recalled the time I'd read aloud from *Man's Search for Meaning*, the memoir of psychiatrist and Auschwitz survivor Viktor Frankl, a book that had helped sustain Rubin Carter through his years behind bars. Mid-passage, I exploded in tears, surprising myself no less than my audience of perplexed friends, and I couldn't continue reading. I now feared the detonation and deluge that would inevitably ensue should this Holocaust door be reopened.

Lindy wisely said I would regret not coming and encouraged me to overcome my apprehension. Unforgettable for her was the incident in the middle of one night at her condo. I got up to go to the bathroom and fainted. All my weight landed on my right foot and I was sure I'd broken it. I hobbled quietly back to bed. When Lindy awoke the next morning, I simply said, "You might need to drive me to Emergency."

"What? And you didn't wake me?"

Not acknowledging when I experienced pain or discomfort was a behavioural pattern that Lindy had already noticed. She wondered if I reflexively downplayed my own suffering because it did not register on the scale of what my parents must have endured. But this injury went beyond the pale, and my silence spoke volumes of why I needed that Holocaust door reopened. Lindy invited my oldest brother, Abe, to the gallery as well. I decided, what the hell.

At the event, I spoke to Stanley Zukerman, who looked like a middle-aged version of the boy he had been in my grade nine class at Wilson Heights Junior High School. He was now president of the Wierzbniker Society.

"Of course, you've read Browning's new book?" Before a "who?" could pass my lips, Stanley continued, "Christopher Browning. Holocaust history specialist. His book is full of your father's words."

"That's impossible. My father's been dead since 1985."

"He was a witness at a war crimes trial. His sworn testimony is on the record."

A heavy drumbeat penetrated the sudden silence in the room, and everyone appeared to be moving in slow motion. Blood thumped so hard against my temples that my skull was a dam about to burst. Visions of grey matter splattered over the gallery's white-painted walls, Lindy having to clean up the bloody mess. I struggled to pull myself together.

"The book — ?"

"*Remembering Survival*. About Wierzbnik during the war."

I was aware my father had gone to Germany in 1970 to testify at a trial. As usual, he offered few details and, as I had already moved out of our family home, my thoughts were elsewhere. One thing he'd said, though, I've never forgotten. Sometime after returning to Canada, he'd told me about a man, some sort of former Nazi commandant, who, upon observing my father walk into the courtroom, reacted as if seeing a ghost.

"*Herr Schneidermeister, lebst du noch?*" (Master Tailor, you're still alive?)

There'd been a triumphant note in my father's retelling, which made me discount the story, seeing it as yet another example of his boasting that had little to do with the truth. Now I questioned myself. Why wouldn't my father have been honestly and justifiably proud? The fact of his survival meant that his life trumped what this man in the prisoner's dock had tried to do to him. Moreover, in that courtroom, acknowledged as the master tailor he truly was, my father was finally going to be heard.

But not by me. At least, not then.

I scrambled to get a copy of Browning's book. It would be a revelation and spark further revelations. It would help me puzzle together a story, my story, my family's story. It would alter my perception of my parents and the influence of their buried trauma on my life and on my brothers' lives. And it would inspire me to write this book, something my father had promised we would eventually do.

Most unexpectedly, it would bring my parents back to me, and me to them....

1

Palmerston

NOISE FROM THE NEXT ROOM PENETRATES MY semi-sleep. The sounds emanating from the kitchen are not of food preparation, but of adults playing poker and conversing over cigarettes and a bottle of Canadian Club *bronfn* (whisky). My younger brother David stirs in his crib. We're ensconced in my parents' bedroom, which should've been the dining room had the house not had so many inhabitants. The chatter is muffled, whispers in a secret language punctuated by outbursts of laughter.

"Sha! Di yinglech shlofn."

Someone is telling the others to keep the noise down because we boys are sleeping. I understand the Yiddish but when they switch to Polish, I'm lost. I think I hear references to naughty body parts. I strain but can't make out anything more. They don't want me to hear. It sounds sexy, the hushed tones, the not wanting the young ones to know. I sense the subject matter harkens back to darker times, although the darkness is lifted by raucous hilarity. The aromatic smoke seeps in through the crack under the door and lulls me back to sleep. This scene is among my earliest memories, and I wish I knew more about it.

Turquoise tattoos, ever-present but never mentioned, marked the forearms of the adults who populated my Toronto childhood home, all of whom seemed to have met in the old country at a camp named Bergen-Belsen. They called it a *lager*, which was neither a type of beer nor like any summer camp I would come to know. All I could gather was that it was a place where relationships were born. Later I was to learn it was the concentration camp where Anne Frank had died.

My parents owned the three-storey, semi-detached house at 591 Palmerston Avenue and rented out rooms to other green-horns who, like them, were war survivors from Europe, inked with the indelible numbers. I fondly remember Mina Binsztok, who was like a kind maiden aunt to me and roomed on the second floor. She had a tattoo, as did the Hungarian Deutsches, a married couple also on the second floor, next to the house's only bathroom we all shared.

A succession of families lived on the third floor. Soon after my father purchased the house, Yankel (Jacob), my father's youngest brother, his wife, Sallah (Sara), and their son, Alf, came to occupy one room on the third floor. Uncle Srulec (Israel), my father's younger brother, and his wife, Basha (Betty), were in the other room, all having newly arrived from Sweden. This living arrangement lasted three years, until Srulec bought a house on Euclid Avenue and all five of them moved there. The Gulas then moved in: Faygaleh, who baked the most delicious lemon meringue pies; her husband, Henyek; and their daughter, Gloria. So did Halene Krozman, who was Mom's distant cousin. Her exit came when she married Max Naiman. I would later babysit their son, who was a terror.

One time I entered the bathroom and saw Mrs. Deutsch naked in the tub, her turquoise markings appearing like veins on pale skin, as she clutched her pendulous breasts and shrieked. I skedaddled red-faced out of there wondering not about the tattoo but about the size of her boobies and whether door locks were a new country invention that took getting used to.

My father, Rachmil's, number was A-19121; my mother, Luba's, A-14239. Had you asked me when I was a child to recite the numerals on their forearms, I would not have been able to. Not that I consciously avoided the tattoos but I did not pay them any mind, let alone try to verbalize them. Having never heard them voiced, I didn't know if you should pronounce each digit individually or combine them, like "A, nineteen, one twenty-one." Or is it an unwieldy, formal "A, nineteen thousand one hundred and twenty-one"? Rubin "Hurricane" Carter's prison number, 45472, which I would come to know by heart, was always for me a string of individual numerals, although I do remember Rube tossing off "forty-five, four, seventy-two" as if it were an oft-used combination to a Dudley lock.

The ubiquity of number tattoos in the world I was born into was unremarkable, and I tacitly acceded to their invisibility. Maybe it was some secondary sexual characteristic that materialized with puberty, like hair around your penis. And you never mentioned that.

Our brick house occupied the southeast corner of Palmerston Avenue and London Street. Its garage, made of wood painted the deep Toronto green that was so popular in the city in the fifties, sat on London Street. A wooden fence, also deep green, linked the garage to the house and hid from view the small backyard and its sagging clothesline. My mother would do laundry in the basement in her prized possession, a Westinghouse wringer washer that filled and emptied through rubber hoses running to and from an oversized sink. (A second sink on the right she sometimes filled with water and an enormous live carp before it was killed, gutted, and ground up for gefilte fish — a slaughter I thankfully never witnessed.) My mother would haul the laundry up the steep steps from the basement, across the large kitchen, her silhouette reflected in its glossy red ceiling, and out through the dilapidated dark space they called a summer kitchen, which seemed to have been time-warped from a prewar shtetl and attached to the house like an afterthought. It was jerry-built from recycled barnwood and usually arrayed with *heymishe* (homey) concoctions like *galleh* (calf's foot jelly) cooling in oversized rectangular metal pans. Down a few steps, Luba and her bundle of the freshly washed would at last emerge into the dappled sunlight of the backyard where sheets, towels, socks, and my father's paisley boxer shorts would be snapped back into shape, pegged, and left to flap in the breeze and dry.

A tall chimney on our house was topped with a terra cotta crown that had holes through which the furnace's smoke puffed. I would not have noticed this clay appendage had I not found it one October day, its nearly two-foot length lying sideways on the ground like a fallen soldier, after being toppled by Hurricane Hazel. I don't recall having heard the wind, but I remember the reticence and tentativeness of the inhabitants of the house, having emerged into the calm with me in tow the day following the iconic storm, amazed there was so little damage.

"Got in himl! Aza vint!" (Heavens! Such a wind!)

"Mir hobn's ibergelebt, got tsu danken." (We survived it, thank God.)

"Dank beser a hoyz fun tsigl geboyt!" (Better to thank a house built from bricks!)

The bulk of the chimney remained erect, along with the stalwart horse chestnut at the front and the maple at the side of the property. But leaves had left the trees in droves to mat and moulder on the water-drenched earth, except for a vermilion one that adhered to the fallen soldier's cheek in an extended farewell kiss.

Completing the block, around the corner were two semi-detached houses on London Street. Next to them, a laneway that ran north and south parallel to Palmerston, and then a police station, Station 11, straddling the corner of Markham Street. There was a stable at the back, where neighbourhood kids would congregate to stroke and sniff the horses, their hairy hides emitting odours that provided a dank base note to the acrid turds they plopped onto their straw beds or left on roadways behind them. In those days, horses were everywhere in this part of the city, not just resting in stalls or at work under mounted constables. Milk and ice would be delivered by horse-drawn carts. I remember ornate carved iron troughs on the corner of Bloor and Bathurst where horses could have a refreshing sip. I remember, too, the oft-told tales of my brother Charlie escaping into the road as a toddler and stuffing his mouth with horse turds.

Toronto's diversity today was already evident in Palmerston's mixed bag of families in the 1950s: an intermingling of Canadians and Displaced Persons, DPs as the new immigrants were derogated. My best friend, Teddy, was blond and his older

brother, Ricky, a redhead. Hair colour other than dark brown
or black was treasured by my mother as a trumpet of non-
Jewishness, always worthy of note. These French-Canadian
boys lived five houses down with their parents, the DesLauriers,
and their grandmother, Parker. Every Sunday, they attended
St. Peter's Catholic Church the next block over on Markham
Street. The property at St. Peter's runs all the way to Bathurst
Street, a stretch perfect for playing hide-and-seek and tag, with
high fences to clamber over and nooks and crannies to hide in,
although our games were sometimes interrupted.

"Good afternoon, Father," my friends would intone upon
seeing a cassock-clad priest walk by. I soon copied their greet-
ing, calling the priests "Father," but unlike my friends, would
seldom receive a "My son," in return.

I loved sneaking into the church, a place of mystery —
exotic, thick with otherworldly incense, and dark, save for the
brightly coloured statues of people in various poses of pain.
They looked up or down but never straight at you, which was
good because I did not want my unschooled efforts at genu-
flecting and crossing myself to be observed by insiders. I
wanted to fit into this theatrical world where people acted out
prescripted roles and the purpose of objects was known only
to the initiated. The fonts of holy water held particular fascin-
ation as did the small wooden box with a slot on the wall in
the entryway in which alms for the poor were dropped. Didn't
know what alms were but if they were anything like arms, I
longed for their embrace.

My urge to find where I belonged was stoked by a feeling of having no place in my own home, the middle son of
five boys, merely an extra in a long list of *dramatis personae*
that included numerous renters connected to my parents by an

invisible shared past. I was easily overlooked in the competing stage business of raised voices, clutched hearts, flailing arm gestures, slaps, and tears. Weekends, when all the tenants were off work, were the most tumultuous. Foremost was the clamour of foreign tongues, a veritable Babel under one roof. The first language of my parents and the tenants was Yiddish, which my brothers and I understood but didn't speak. We would answer back in English, and this is how they would learn the language of the new country. When my parents didn't want us to understand, they'd resort to Polish, their secret tongue.

Whatever the language, in our house it wasn't actually spoken but *geshrign*: commands barked, prohibitions issued, and histrionics displayed. "*Gey, ver gehargt!*" Literally, "Go, get yourself killed!" a less benign equivalent of "Go jump in the lake!" or "Get lost, kid!" This was an injunction my parents issued when at wit's end, which was often. No polite, casual, tempered conversation here.

Hungarian was added to the cacophony by the Deutsches, who frequently had an issue with the house's single bathroom either monopolized by one of us or a big fish swimming in the tub, or because there was no hot water, which my father was challenged to redress.

"*Hèt dollar hetente fizetni — ezèrt?*" (Seven dollars a week I pay — for this?)

In the kitchen, meanwhile, my mother would be bathing my youngest brother in the sink, with an assist from Mina. Or she'd be stuffing chicken livers into a silver metal grinder, cranking out worms of meat for chopped liver while nursing something sweet, like a honey cake, in the oven. Or she'd be trying to prevent us boys, vocally or with any means at hand, from killing one another. Usually, it was all these activities at once.

No meals were served on Saturdays. Food was grabbed on the fly as the urge arose. My older brothers, busy and self-absorbed, each going his own direction out to play regardless of the weather or hunkered down to teach the younger boys a lesson for messing with their stuff.

I recall the time Charlie waved in our faces a purple velvet Seagram's Crown Royal drawstring bag in which he kept his prized cat's-eye marbles and boulders. He threatened to kill anyone who touched them. Although I had my own collection of marbles, I coveted one of Charlie's, a translucent, pale gold sphere that shimmered with tiny blue flecks like stars afloat in the Milky Way. I was willing to trade him several of my alleys for it. Charlie scoffed. He called it a rare beauty and said it would cost me all my marbles, the boulders and the cat's-eyes. He wouldn't budge. It was a deal I had to decline.

In the winter, my mother would beg Charlie to take me with him to Christie Pits, where sliding down the park's hills on flattened cardboard refrigerator boxes was a favourite activity. Charlie would always ignore her entreaties and take off without me, preferring to hang out with his own friends unencumbered by a kid three years his junior. "But he's your brother!" didn't count for much. Disappointed, I was determined not to rely on him and eventually figured out how to get there myself. Abie, the oldest, was rarely around, either studying or working, and Harvey had not yet been born.

Sometimes I would wrangle David — at two years younger, closest to me in age — into doing creative gymnastics. I'd lie on my back, feet flat on the floor, knees bent, and get him to balance himself in a high plank over me, facing my feet, his hands resting on my knees while I held his legs aloft. We'd assume this position, then try it each using only one hand, then shifting to another statuesque arrangement, the structure collapsing with our laughter and devolving into some seriously loud wrestling and even louder intervention. If Charlie were around, he'd want in on the action, and someone would end up getting hurt.

Although my father was often miserly with words, he donated generously to the household mayhem. First of all, with his belt — its coruscating silver buckle and its whoosh and slap as it whisked the air and sprawled to a stop on bare skin, a sleight-of-hand that conjured from its recipient (at the very least) an "Ow! Ow! Ow! Ow! Ow!" followed by a flood of waterworks. Secondly, with his scowling demeanour that never failed to strike fear and dread in his treading little angels.

Then there was his obsession with our rotary dial phone, a heavy black contraption that barely fit the Lilliputian table in the narrow hallway at the foot of the stairs. There were different ring tones, combinations of long and short rings that would signal the intended party, but my father would pick up the receiver no matter who the call was for, stand there, and listen. The phone would not even have to ring and still it seemed to call to him like a silent siren, prompting much movement — up and down in chairs and in and out of rooms — and the raising of his voice. Clad in boxer shorts and a wife beater, he would repeatedly repair to the hallway where the phone lay in wait for him. Sometimes I would follow and watch him pick up the receiver and shout into it.

"Hallo! Hallo! Who iz dis? Rakhmil iz do. Vos vil ich? Ch'vil makhn a call. Shoyn tsvansik minit vart ich!" (Rachmil here. What do I want? I wanna make a call. I've been waiting twenty minutes already!)

The telephone party line, shared by all in the house as well as some neighbours, was for him no party but part of life's daily frustration — *tsuris* he'd call it — to be borne in silence or exorcized with anger.

* * *

If my home life was open-ended chaos, then the DesLauriers' was all ritual and order, especially on Saturdays, when there were actual sit-down meals. My friends' repast was pork hot dogs in fluffy white buns, so much tastier and pinker than the dun-coloured bland kosher beef ones (Chicago brand or Shopsy's, both equally dreadful) that would roll off slices of rye bread at home. One notable Saturday I was invited to stay for lunch and sat at the kitchen table with Teddy and Ricky, munching joyously. Mrs. DesLauriers (her first name, as I recall, was Joan), a perfectly aproned June Cleaver, was washing dishes at the sink, her back to us.

"Who's smacking their lips?"

The brothers looked askance at me. I busied myself slathering more mustard on a hot dog, conscious I had done something wrong but unsure what the big deal was. Didn't my father *patshke* his lips while eating as a sign of great enjoyment and a compliment to the cook?

I tried to make less noise but to no avail. Mrs. D turned around and asked her sons where their manners were, reminding them they had to chew with their mouths closed. News to me. But I was too embarrassed to fess up, and Ricky and Teddy, too well-mannered to point fingers.

Saturday night at the DesLauriers' was bath night. The boys would share a tub of hot water and their mother would scrub them for church the next day. Such an orderly, *goyishe* world! I kept hoping to be invited to participate in that rite as well, but it never came to pass. What happened at Christmas in 1958, when I was eight years old, was for the ages. Usually, all the DesLauriers would spend Christmas Day together in church, but that year, Teddy had some childhood ailment (or did this have something to do with his eye, the one he went blind in after another kid tossed a firecracker that accidentally exploded near Teddy's face?) and had to stay home. I kept him company the entire day and got to share in the unwrapping then the playing with a humongous number of presents: the Dinky Toys, the Slinky, the Etch A Sketch, the Lionel model train. It didn't matter that there were no presents under the DesLauriers' tree for me. I prayed for Teddy to get sick every Christmas.

2

Reading and Bleeding

I LONGED TO BE GROWN UP LIKE MY OLDER brothers. Reading and writing, which Abie and Charlie seemed adept at, were markers that announced to the world that you had arrived. I have a vivid memory of sitting alone at the kitchen table with a brightly coloured alphabet book. I had not yet begun school and couldn't read. But I was given a pencil and some paper and told to practise printing the alphabet by copying the shapes of the letters. I got stuck on the lowercase *g*, trying to replicate the way it was ornately printed with closed loops at the top and bottom, joined together by a curved line on the left side, and a curlicue that jutted out to the right from the top of the letter. As further complication, the loops had blank oval shapes in their centre, the top one with the oval running vertically, the bottom one horizontally. I struggled on my own but no matter how hard I tried, I couldn't get it to look like the letter in the book. I asked my father for help. When I finally got his attention, he shrugged and told me to ask "Avrum," which is what he called my oldest brother. But Abie was out on his dark green Raleigh bike delivering orders for the local pharmacy, earning some pocket change and the approval of my father. Abie always had important things to do, following a path my father had paved for him. That there was a simple way to write the letter *g*, I eventually figured out on my own.

In my preliterate days, I used to spend hours on our porch perusing my older brothers' comic books and pretending I could read what was in the balloons and the text at the bottom of each frame. I would flip a page, pause for a suitable length of time, then flip another and another until I reached the back page. I'd close the book with a triumphant flourish and look around nonchalantly to see if anyone had noticed.

A couple of doors down from the DesLauriers lived two girls, one named Linda and her younger sister, Donna, about my age, very pretty, with sticklike skinny legs I thought were shapely. One of the older boys on the street had watched my comic book charade and coaxed me into writing the older sister a special note. He had to spell out all the words for me. If I remember correctly, the missive went like this: "I am going to pull your dick hairs out by the roots." I was excited to have written my first letter, even if I didn't know exactly what it meant. My note, folded in half with the name "Linda" scrawled on one side, was left on the girls' porch. Its reception was not a warm one. I ended up being mortified, vilified as a nasty little boy. A short time later, the girls moved out of the neighbourhood. If there was a connection, I wouldn't be surprised.

Next to Linda's house lived an old man who smoked nothing but Sweet Caporal filterless cigarettes. Often he would corral us kids to run up to Carruther's, the corner druggist, to buy him a deck of smokes. He was always talking about "old bugger" this and that, and everyone but me would laugh. When I found out that buggery was illegal, I couldn't imagine why. I thought a bugger had something to do with catching insects.

Across the street lived another two sisters, one named Carol. They didn't have a mother, and the sisters would have to do the laundry and cook for their dad on a stove they needed to climb a chair to reach. His dinner had to be on the table by the time he got home from work or there was hell to pay. Their house was a worn Cinderella cottage covered in peeling burgundy tarpaper shingles, its saving grace a cherry tree out back that I would scale for early summer treats. We would feast on the bounty until our stomachs ached.

Next door to them was an old woman who had a wood stove in her kitchen. I would, from time to time, get on my hands and knees and scrub her hardwood floors with steel wool and turpentine then apply paste wax, which had an intoxicating scent I couldn't get enough of. After letting the wax dry for about twenty minutes and getting my nostrils saturated, I would skate over each section several times with a soft, clean rag underfoot, buffing the floors to a high satiny sheen. Twenty-five cents for my efforts was the payment, in effect doubling my allowance.

Directly across the street from us lived the Adelmans, including Howard, who was older than me and a close friend of Abie's. Howard would go on to be a founder of Rochdale College and, later, of Operation Lifeline, the private sponsorship program that enabled over 100,000 Vietnamese refugees to settle in Canada. The Adelmans moved out when I was still pretty young and a German family moved in. I befriended one of the kids, an Aryan poster boy about my age, named Manfred. He and his older brother had amazing bicycles that looked like BMWs, high-tech racers that had accompanied them from Germany, one electric blue, the other a pale green.

One Saturday, I went to the movies with Manfred. I used to see a double feature matinee every Saturday afternoon at one of the three movie houses located around the corner on Bloor Street: the Alhambra, the Metro, or the Midtown (now the Hot Docs Ted Rogers Cinema). My allowance was just enough to cover the fifteen-cent admission and the ten-cent box of popcorn. *The Young Philadelphians* was playing, a lawyer drama starring Paul Newman. As I was only eight years old, I was more interested in playing with Manfred. I stuck my hand down his pants and felt his boner. Later, in the alleyway behind my house, we pulled down our pants and did the same to each other. I was fascinated by his penis, which was uncircumcised and had a crook in it. I was holding his, he was holding mine, feeling warm, when suddenly Mrs. DesLauriers's head appeared over the fence.

"Have you seen Te...?" Her jaw dropped. "What in God's name are you doing?"

We turned as red as our dicks. We didn't answer — we just raised our trousers and scrambled out of there.

Kitty-corner across the street lived the Katzes. Sometimes I'd play with Itsik (Ian), who was my age. His mother never liked him to stray too far from the house, but she also wasn't thrilled about our playing inside, where the living room provided the only available space. Mrs. Katz would give us a few minutes then come flying hawk-eyed into the room.

"Are you picking your nose?" she'd ask me, as if she'd heard something untoward.

"No," I'd invariably reply.

In disbelief, she'd check to see if we had smeared boogers on her plastic-covered sofa. Even when her inspection proved fruitless, she'd ask us to leave. On the way out, we had to pass the upright piano that was jammed into their hallway. Ian told me his mother used to play, although he'd never heard her. He asked me if I could play.

"I dunno," I said. "I never tried."

The next time I was there, I tried, only to discover my playing didn't amount to much more than a snake charmer's tune I'd heard in cartoons.

A few doors up the street lived the Friedmans. They had a furniture store in Kensington Market. Maneel (Larry) was a playmate, although I also knew his older sister, Hindy. Once I went with Larry to a Zionist place where young Jews were hanging out. I felt like a complete outsider. I didn't understand the fervour for a land called Israel, a country my parents rarely mentioned. I was firmly rooted in my childhood landscape.

Beauty was everywhere for me in the natural world. It was in the whirligig maple seeds and sleek horse chestnuts I gathered from the trees on my street, in the fruit that grew in neighbours' yards, the tart Montmorency cherries, crisp apples, shapely pears. My hungry senses seldom had far to go to find satiety. Even the witch's house one street over had a purple plum tree, its forbidden fruit a treasure that took derring-do to raid. I knew the neighbourhood well, and high on the list of important things to know was the location of fragrant French lilacs and tall, fruit-scented tulips that could be admired, if not stolen, on the way to school in spring; or, in late summer, how to liberate surprises from milkweed pods, how to produce a frisson from the friction of fingers over the velvet of hollyhocks that buttressed at odd angles the dilapidated fences in the laneway behind our house. Chocolate chenille caterpillars, praying mantises, garter snakes with stripes that slithered from tip to tail were ever-present and bountiful signs of enchantment, of the earth's fullness, of its busyness and never-ending ability to delight.

Even in winter — especially in winter — the world was dazzling. The wand of the snow turned it crisp, white, diamantine. Best of all was the quiet — until you took that first step, that is, and the crunch underfoot cracked the still air — and your breath was dragon visible in the still air, and it was so cold, inhaling had to be done in tiny, shallow increments. The blue of the sky earned its name on those clear, frigid January days that rolled on and on, blue over white, blue, blue, sky blue without end.

When my friends weren't around, I'd play by myself. Favourite activities were collecting seeds and nuts and squirrelling them away in mason jars. In the spring, I would gather the light green helicoptery propeller pods that floated down from maple trees. I would eject their fragrant seeds into jars, building up a huge collection that had a distinctive piquant green tang but were otherwise useless. In the early fall, it would be horse chestnuts, those spikey chartreuse sputniks that grew on a number of trees on our street. I'd split these open to reveal a gleaming, hard brown nut. I'd bore a hole through some of the largest and densest ones, tie a shoelace through the hole, and whip them around like weaponized yo-yos, trying to smash a friend's similarly strung chestnut. The conker that remained intact would be a kinger, reigning momentarily until it was usurped. However strong the demand for more chestnuts, the supply seemed endless.

Blood, too, was in abundance in our little section of Palmerston. It was literally a bloody place. The corner where we lived had no stop signs, so car crashes at the intersection were not uncommon. The screech of tires, the thud and crunch of metal, and the shatter of glass would have us running instantly from the house. My mother once sent me back inside to retrieve towels from the bathroom. I watched from the porch as she tended to the accident victim, holding our freshly laundered towels against his blood-soaked head until the ambulance arrived.

There was even a multiple murder on Palmerston Square, a few doors up from the Friedmans'. A man had shot his wife, his children, and himself. Larry had managed to sneak into the house before the police arrived. He came running out and called a local radio station with a news tip. I recall being excited to hear Larry's voice on the radio. He said he saw blood everywhere. The street was cordoned off for the whole day. I later learned that this family had recently arrived from Europe. The father, they said, was despondent. He'd been trying to get his family to Israel but for some reason they weren't able to go.

I asked my mother about it and her response was silence. I pressed her. Didn't she know the family? She feigned ignorance. Denial was her default setting. Anything involving loss of life, she would go out of her way to keep from us, if not lie outright about it. I remember overhearing her once whispering to another survivor standing at our front door, about the death of a landsman's son I had once met. I later mentioned to my mother how shocked I was he'd killed himself.

"What are you talking?" She insisted it was an accident caused by an unlucky fall.

"Well, what was he doing at the edge of the roof in the first place?"

I never did receive an answer.

One day in our kitchen with the blood red ceiling, Abie and Charlie were getting into their usual tussle, pummelling each other and winding up in a ball of fury that rumbled across the kitchen like a Tasmanian devil. My mother yelled at them but couldn't get them to stop. She picked up a fork and hurled it across the kitchen table. It landed and stuck in Abie's forearm, standing straight up. There was some blood, not a lot, oozing out of the four pinpoints where the prongs had pricked the skin. In one bold move, my mother yanked the fork out. Abie fainted. This is the guy who went on to fulfill my parents' wishes and become a doctor.

Another time in the sanguinary kitchen, Charlie pitched a wooden toy train, striking the back of my head and setting off a gusher of blood. As usual, my mother was there to save the day. She got a bottle of iodine out of the cupboard, then held me real tight as she poured the iodine on the open wound. I writhed. I screamed. A lot. I would tell future barbers not to cut off too much in the back, that there was a scar and I didn't want it to show.

So much (for the) blood.

* * *

The police station on London Street had great features in addition to the stable that made us want to hang out. A waist-high brick ledge ran around the building at a forty-five degree angle to the sky, a surface perfect for serving rubber handballs; and adjacent to the building, a large lawn on which we could race, catch, and smash balls against the brick wall above the ledge, keeping volleys going forever. It was a perfect space, too, for simple games like Red Light, Green Light or rougher ones like Red Rover and British Bulldog. Here we also invented our own games, like Shoot 'Em Down, which had us charging toward a shooter with an imaginary gun, getting shot, stumbling, falling, and dying, the winner being the one with the most creative death throes.

Playing handball there with the DesLauriers brothers one day, I missed an easy shot.

"Oh shit!"

As I ran toward the edge of the lawn to retrieve the ball, I noticed that a police cruiser had stopped, its driver's elbow protruding out the rolled-down window.

"Come here."

"Me?"

"Yeah. You."

I approached the lone officer gingerly.

"What did you say?"

"Nothing."

"Well, I heard something."

Silence.

"What was it?"

I looked down at my running shoes. Not Keds, but I could still fly in these, couldn't I?

"Oh shit," I whispered.

"You called me a shit."

"No, I didn't."

"I know what I heard."

He asked me where I lived and I nodded in the direction of my house.

"Hop in the car."

He leaned over and opened the front passenger door of the bright yellow cruiser. Reluctantly, I got in. My handball chums were staring at me, incredulous. I had to give the cop my address. He drove at an excruciatingly slow pace the few metres around the corner to Palmerston and parked, facing the wrong direction, in front of my house. I didn't look up, but I know where the eyes of neighbours, especially those of Mrs. Katz, were focused.

We got out of the car, and I followed the officer up the front steps. He hammered on the door. My mother answered, a look of fear shading her eyes. We went into the living room. All of us remained standing. The cop, nearly touching the ceiling even after removing his cap, told my mother I had a mouth on me and needed to watch my language. I tried to explain but she cut me short. She looked up to the constable.

"Tenks very much, Mister Officer. Again dis will never heppn."

As soon as the cop left, my mother slapped me hard on the mouth.

"Efn nisht dem pisk!" (Shut your big mouth!)

But that was nothing compared to what my father and his belt had to say when he got home.

* * *

Three crystal bowls, weighty and ornately cut, anchored the white lace runner on my parents' dresser, never anything in them, just there, sparkling and out of place in the bedroom with the light-coloured veneer furniture set. The crystal arrived in the new country with my parents. I can't imagine what convoluted logistics preceded their landing on these shores, nor why these objects that had originally been sand were important. There was also a Dresden Porcelain piece, a rococo figurine of a woman in a voluminous eighteenth-century gown that looked even more like a fish out of water. On display beside her, a framed sepia photo of a young man with piercing, dark eyes that hinted of light. My mother never spoke of him nor of any of her family from the old country. All she would say was that this was her brother, who, one morning during the war, left home to get a newspaper and never returned. I had a feeling that I reminded my mother of him, not that she said so. Maybe it was the way she frequently remarked on my eyes, noting with delight how black and sparkling they were.

My mother's eyes were something else. I always thought she was beautiful, with deep-set dark brown eyes that flanked a thin, aquiline nose. Her eyelids were almost completely invisible when her eyes were open. She loved to wear blue eyeshadow but usually smeared it on too high, a little too close to the eyebrows. When asked how her makeup looked (she always asked me, never my dad or my brothers), I would find it impossible not to nod in approval and say, "Nice."

There was a jewellery store on Bloor Street, around the corner from where we lived. I often looked in the window, my child eyes attracted to the glitter, alas too expensive for my budget, in which a nickel's worth of bologna at the local butcher's was an extravagance. One day, there was a small mountain of compact, neatly wrapped boxes with a sign that read "Surprise Package only 50 cents." My mother's birthday was approaching, and I thought carefully about getting her one of these surprise packages, which were already wrapped and with, no doubt, something amazing inside. Still, I felt uncomfortable about taking a chance on buying blind. I decided to sleep on it.

The next day when I came by to gaze upon the mountain of wrapped treasures, I noticed in another window a bracelet of purple, pink, and blue stones that gleamed like the multi-hued quartz I'd seen in the geology section at the Royal Ontario Museum. The colour and radiance of the stones took my breath away. I went into the store and asked the clerk how much the bracelet cost. The man turned over the tag.

"One dollar."

I wasn't surprised that this thing of beauty was so expensive. He kindly lifted it out of the window for me to hold to the light.

"Can I buy it on layaway?" I asked. If I put down a deposit, they would hold it for me. I gave the man my allowance quarter and promised to pay it off in three weeks. No movies and popcorn for me.

Every week I returned with another quarter until the purchase was done. I had them gift wrap it in a navy velvet box and tied with a matching satin ribbon. I couldn't wait to see my mother's face when I gave it to her.

"What's this?" she asked, as if it were an annoyance if not a trick. I told her to go ahead and open it.

She tugged at the ribbon, which unravelled easily, opened the box, and gave a little laugh. She held the bracelet up and the light came pouring through, shimmering like a soap bubble in the sun.

"You shouldn't have done this."

"I wanted to get you something special for your birthday."

"You wasted your money." Her dismissive tone sucked the air from the room. "What am I going to do with it?"

I begged her to try it on. Instead, she put it back in the box and closed the lid.

"You don't like it?"

"What's not to like?"

I hadn't realized that gift-giving could be so fraught with danger. I left the room and cried.

3

Place Holders

TIMES AWAY FROM HOME WERE TREASURED.
Overnight stays, especially in hospital, felt safe and luxurious.
Some of my fondest boyhood memories were at the Hospital for
Sick Children in a bed all to myself, no brother beside me, and
with not one but two crisp white sheets and starched WASPy
nurses who fawned over and showered me with exotic fare like
butterscotch pudding and toothpaste powder.

I was sickly as a child, but now that I think about it, I don't
know if I had more health issues than any normal kid, except
maybe in regard to eating. My mother was obsessed with food
and eating. Indeed, her whole existence orbited around food
shopping, meal preparation, cooking, and feeding. I can't imagine how much our family would consume — let's just say,

bushels. Luckily for my mother, there was a walk-in pantry off our kitchen where she could store extra provisions.

The only effective weapon I had against my mother was to not eat. I often pushed my plate away at the table as a valiant act of resistance. This would drive her into a pique of solicitousness and wide-open menus, unappealing except for the occasional French toast and the *kreplach*, her arsenal of ravioli-like triangles of squishy dough with a hint of ground meat inside, which, when all else failed, she assembled from scratch to make chicken soup palatable for me. All the more and nonetheless, I was a skinny child, and my mother would constantly fret about getting me to put on weight. *Es oyf!* (Eat up!) was her *cri de coeur.*

In that regard, two memories stand out. One was a hospital stay to have my appendix removed when I was around six. I don't recall having had appendicitis or anything like that. I do remember being in bed on a ward at Sick Kids and asking my parents why I was there.

"You're going to have an operation."

"What for?"

"To make you eat more."

And so I had my appendix removed. Still have the scar to show for it, a three-inch slash running on a forty-five-degree angle up toward the top right tip of my pelvis.

But it was years before my appetite improved.

Memory Two. I found myself, toward the end of grade two, separated from my friends. I'd been sent to a school held out of doors in High Park. It was a health school that would help me gain weight. That's what they told me, and I sometimes wonder if this place really existed or if it was a nightmare prompted by my mother like a heavy meal before sleep.

Classes were held in classrooms with no roofs. That was pretty cool. What wasn't cool was having to take a streetcar out of my Palmerston Avenue neighbourhood along Bloor Street to High Park (this was a decade before the Bloor subway line) not only every weekday but Saturday as well. Extended school hours made for no time to be with my playmates. I was alone and unhappy.

The worst part was the dining hall where we would parade in, single file. We'd have to stand at the wooden tables, say the Lord's Prayer and sing "God Save the Queen" before we could eat. Not that eating was any great shakes. The food was goyish and unfamiliar. The macaroni and cheese had the sort of texture and putrid smell that made me question whether the meal had already been devoured and this was its second go-round. The pièce de résistance was the cod liver oil capsule, a perfect amber sphere neatly nestled beside every place setting. That first day we were commanded to take it, I had no reason not to comply. I put it into my mouth, bit in, and proceeded to gag on the viscous fish liquid inside. Nothing I drank adequately masked the oceanic taste. After repeating this misery for several days, I finally decided that to keep from puking, I would palm the capsule instead. No one ever told me you were supposed to swallow it whole.

There came a time when I'd had enough. I don't know if it was the lousy food or something special happening on Palmerston that day that I longed to be part of, but I took off from my classroom and bolted into the woods. I guess I didn't cover my escape too well because in short order I was being pursued down ravines and up hillsides. I darted through the underbrush, my heart and skinny legs pumping. I kept looking back over my left shoulder. Two grown men were gaining on me. If I could just make it to Bloor Street! Dead leaves crunched loud underfoot, twigs and branches snapped back hard, scratching my face and hands. But the faster I ran, the closer my pursuers got. I gasped for breath and heard their panting chugging ever louder. Terror and hopelessness rose in my gut when I was snatched up, legs flailing, then subdued and summarily escorted to the principal's office off the dreaded mess hall.

I don't believe I was asked to explain my flight. In any event, I was speechless, mute about the cod liver oil capsules and the unfairness of being imprisoned while my friends ran free. Punishment was called for.

The principal opened a cabinet, then a drawer. He lifted out a wide wad of leather, using both hands as if to make a presentation to the Queen of England. It was the kind of strop barbers used to sharpen their straight razors to hairsplitting acuteness. I'm not sure how many swats I took on my open palm, but I think it was ten.

God bless Wikipedia. Here it is, "High Park Forest School." I wasn't dreaming.

Created in the early 1900s, "it was initially a place for children with tuberculosis but through the years it became a summer school for underprivileged and/or undernourished children.... [who] attended the school from May 1 to October 31 to augment their education and also get good nutritious foods and exercise to help them become healthy."[1] As far as I was concerned, my health returned that fall when I returned to my chums at Palmerston Avenue Public School.

I now live near High Park. The Forest School no longer exists but the main building, which contained the mess hall and the principal's office, is still there. Occasionally, I go jogging past it — last time there were two women in Lululemons doing yoga on the verandah — and I remember with equanimity what went on there as if it were a Victorian tale I had read long ago, something that had happened to a David Copperfield, not to me. The hills and valleys I had once traversed in breathless terror are now benign landscape, calming, rejuvenating, invigorating. I inhale deeply and continue my easy lope. But abusive treatment is a burden not easily shed. As I stride on that well-worn soil, following the pathways that snake through the trees, more mature and taller now (the trees and me), it's not muscle memory that gives my steps their weight and bounce but the recall, nearly six decades later, of childhood's tender skin.

* * *

Crystal Beach on Lake Erie became a popular haunt in the mid-1950s for Jewish families escaping the heat of the city in summer. Following our family's years of Sunday picnics at High Park, then Toronto Island, then Pontypool near Pickering, the drive to Crystal Beach signalled an expansive move. An amusement park and wooden roller coaster could be found there and a beach with fine sand and shallow sun-warmed water extending far out from shore.

I was young and couldn't yet swim but was enthralled by the broader horizons the world now offered. I wandered into the lake and walked, stride after stride, assuredly toward the sun. I could have pressed on forever, it seemed, but then the bottom fell out and I found myself floating face down, eyes wide open, blissful, buoyant, and drifting in the yellow-green water. A sure hand at the nape of my neck brought my adventure to a sudden end. Snatched out of the water, I was hoisted into the overheated blue air and carried back to land. When we reached the shore, my father set me down and doused my face with lake water as if it were something I sorely needed. His ministration puzzled me then and still does now. I don't know if it was meant as a warning of what could have been my watery grave had he not been present or if it was some kind of homeopathic folk cure, a small dosage of like curing like, a prophylaxis against the perils of straying.

There was another incident when my father's reaction was even more unexpected. I was playing tag with some kids outside our Palmerston house. To escape being "it," I ran up the front steps onto the porch. I cleverly got up on the balustrade and hurled myself to the ground some five or six feet below. Problem was my earthward leap was far from the smooth affair in my mind's eye. I fell forward and landed on my arm, which seemed to penetrate the earth like a plumb line. I tried to raise my arm but it was too heavy and unresponsive, tried to get up but couldn't. My father appeared and saw me prostrate, struggling to lift my eyes to importune him. He moved in closer and I glimpsed first fear then fury reddening his face. He hesitated a moment before he swung his leg back and kicked me. I was his first child born in the new country, bringing him nothing but *tsuris*.

"Ven vet es zayn git?" (When will it be good?)

My father's rhetorical lament was to be uttered many times over the course of his life and, as best I could, I resisted making it my own.

The experience provided perhaps the most cogent proof of a conspiracy against God I had yet uncovered. I became convinced that my parents, indeed all adults, were purposely interfering with my relationship with the Divine Being.

They were trying to turn my world into a less beautiful place, to make me hate and denounce God in the process. It's not that I was religious; it was a phase I was going through. I had been exposed to the Salvation Army and the story of Job and I couldn't help identifying with it. Another proof was furnished by my mother when she found a miniature bible one of the Army's soldiers had given me and freaked that it contained only the New Testament. I marvelled at the tiny print in the inch-square book and begged her not to take it from me, but she did anyway. In the future, I would be cannier and would keep contraband like Christmas tinsel well secreted. I resolved that no matter what atrocious behaviour they came up with, I wouldn't let it jade me.

My father, however, proved to be a formidable foe. In the mid-fifties, we still had a coal furnace in the cellar with one of those terrifying metal doors that could be swung open to reveal a roaring hellfire within. There was also a clothesline running in front of it, strung across the room's length. My father was very strict about our attendance at Hebrew school (from four to six p.m. Monday through Thursday, plus two hours on Sunday morning) and we were equally lax about attending. One day, my father was informed that my older brother Charlie had frequently been absent. This prompted my father to remove his belt as soon as he got home. He swatted Charlie all the way down to the basement and then used the belt to tie him to the clothesline, just inches from the dreaded door and the blazing inferno. Rachmil swore that if Charlie didn't behave, next for him was the oven.

Charlie's attendance at Hebrew school miraculously improved. His relationship with Rachmil also improved. Charlie would grow up to do anything for my father to win his love

My biological family blowing out candles at Abie's Bar Mitzvah, 1959. *From the left*: David, Charlie, Abie, Mom, Harvey, Dad, and me.

and approval, ultimately a gainless quest because the meagre banquet of Dad's love and approval was reserved for number one son, Abie the doctor. In later years, Charlie would often tenderly comb Dad's hair, what little of it there was. Rachmil, who was bald on top, claimed his hair had fallen out from the friction of the Cossack hat he wore in the Russian cavalry. I never believed him, neither that a hat could cause baldness, nor that he was ever a Cossack. What was a Polish Jew doing in the Russian cavalry anyway? None of this fazed Charlie. At five feet eleven, he would tower over my father, who would stand still as a cat, tolerating, enjoying even, the repetition of downward strokes of black plastic teeth against the sides of his skull. It was an odd ritual, this grooming, not least because Rachmil would never leave the house without donning his grey or tan stingy brim fur felt fedora, his side hairs scarcely visible.

My father's violence had a different effect on me.

It made me hate God.

And swear I'd never have children of my own. I was afraid I would turn out like my father.

*　*　*

I, too, skipped Hebrew school, although I was inexplicably spared being tied up beside the furnace in the basement and beaten like a dust-laden rug. I wonder now whether my mother, who seemed to have a softer spot for me, intervened on my behalf or if I had indeed been beaten and suppressed the memory. Today, if anyone raises a hand to me, even in jest, I immediately flinch.

Hebrew school is called *cheyder* in Yiddish; it sounds like "hater," only with something stuck in your throat that you're trying to spit out. Like the Forest School in High Park, I hated it because it separated me from my friends during critical hours after school and on Sunday mornings. I skipped class whenever I could, and when I was present, I was so resentful that I resolved to learn as little as possible. How I learned to read Hebrew given my paltry attentiveness was a miracle akin to the tiny bit of oil of the Maccabees that ended up lasting eight days. Or was it someone else who had the oil? Maybe Jesus with the loaves and fishes might be a better analogy? Or not.

Hebrew school was held on Brunswick Avenue near College Street in a brown brick building with windows that opened onto a fire escape for quick exits. Everything inside was wood, from the desks to the floors to the yardsticks that teachers would use to keep students in line. Even the old TTC Bathurst streetcars that I'd take to get there had wood in them.

I remember one day making a break for it, slipping out an open window and down the fire escape. The powers that be decided I was causing trouble because I was too smart and bored. The solution? Skip me up a grade to challenge me more. As I said, it was a miracle I ever learned anything. But really, it wasn't much. I can't even recite the Hebrew alphabet past *hey*.

My uncle Yankel and his family lived at that time on Euclid Avenue near Ulster, not far from the *cheyder*, with Uncle Srulec and Auntie Basha in a single-family house, continuing to share resources and saving toward self-sufficiency. My uncles worked in an automotive hardware factory owned by the brother of a landsman named Goldhar, who lived across the street from us on Palmerston. At Christmas, there'd be a party at their work that we nephews would attend under the guise of being my uncles' own children. That way we'd get presents: Eaton's boxes with pyjamas, socks, and robes that would tide us over until the following year.

To the Euclid Avenue house we'd go for Passover family Seders, which I looked forward to, especially seeing Auntie Sallah. I always found her a little hipper and more sympatico than my other relatives (was it her years in Sweden after the war?). My cousin Alf, who was born in Sweden and closest to my age, would also be there as well as his younger brother, Howard. (Their sister Gail was born much later.) There was an unspoken rivalry between Alf and me over who got the better marks in school. Now that I think of it, it must have been spoken. Comparisons were always being made. My mother, for example, was reputed to be a better cook than Auntie Sallah. Luba was renowned as a wonderful baker: her honey cake ("So moist!"); apple cake and sugar cookies ("To die for!"). But Auntie Sallah, "She only makes hot dogs." And her home was grimier than Auntie Basha's, whose floors were always "so clean, you could eat off them." How about a fecundity contest? Luba gave birth to five children; Auntie Basha and Uncle Srulec didn't have any kids. A competition also flared between Abie and Neil Berman, a second cousin on my mother's side, which culminated in medical school at the University of Toronto, where Abie graduated second in his class; Neil was first.

I had my own competitive streak. I recall a time in public school when the teacher asked my class a question and gave us until the afternoon to mull it over. My research was a lunchtime phone call to Alf. I asked him what the main export product of Quebec was. I had thought it would be lumber or maple syrup. But Alf corrected me in a tone that conveyed, "What's the matter with you? Everyone knows this!"

"Asbestos," I proudly told my teacher, who made no mention of the mesothelioma that was being unleashed upon the world. No one else in class knew the answer. I couldn't stop smiling, tickled that I had impressed the teacher and had scooped the information from Alf without his knowing how important it was to me.

Even with the competition, I loved the ritual of holidays and sitting around a table with my extended family. The only part of the Seder I didn't like was that Passover usually fell in April during the Stanley Cup playoffs. I wasn't unhappy about missing the playoffs, but my uncles and cousins had become such huge hockey fans that their love of hockey intruded on the Seder festivities. Uncle Yankel's turning on the radio to catch the latest score would shatter the ritual atmosphere. I was more interested in sitting at a large table with the extended family, which was the only time I felt a kind of closeness with my own nuclear one. The Four Questions and the sweet Manischewitz wine were added bonuses. We sang, we laughed, we ate, we escaped, at least temporarily, from Egypt.

Once we got our first TV set in the late fifties, the TV was always on. My aunts used to come over and watch wrestling. They'd sit on the couch, these diminutive women, and shout at the screen, cheering on their favourites like Sweet Daddy Siki, Bobo Brazil, and Bruno Sammartino; and more often than not, decrying bad calls from the referee, which Auntie Basha was particularly adept at.

"Gib im a kope in di beytsim arayn, se kikt der ref nish' tsi!"[2] (Kick him in the nuts, the ref's not looking!)

I picture her pushing her horn-rimmed glasses back onto the bridge of her nose, her rage directed at the flickering black and white images.

"Nu, kakker, shlug shoyn!"[3] (Come on, shitter, hit him already!)

The taste for violence in this tiny, normally self-contained, prim woman made me laugh at first, then scared me. She didn't take kindly to us boys, never speaking to us or acknowledging us directly unless we had sullied her freshly scrubbed floors. Over the years, we didn't have much to do with her and Srulec. They adopted a baby girl named Cori and, it was said, being a mother softened her, if only *a bisl.*

*   *   *

I never knew my grandparents, from either side. Actually, it was more like I didn't know I'd even had grandparents. That's how little my mother and father would speak about their respective parents. When I asked, the subject would be quickly changed. Over the years, I managed to glean that my mother's father was a scholar and a rabbi. But I never found out his name. Or the name of his wife, my maternal grandmother. My father's father I discovered was a tailor named Abraham, and that's who my oldest brother was named after. His wife, my paternal grandmother, her name? What were they like? How did they die? When did they die?

"Freg nisht!" (Don't ask!)

"Were they in the concentration camp with you? Okay, so you've got two brothers, Srulec and Yankel. You have any sisters? Or were you like us, just boys?"

With much badgering and wrangling, an almost inaudible answer.

"Three."

"You had three sisters? Where are they? Are they still alive?"

"No."

"What happened to them?"

This question was answered with silence, as was the following one.

"What were their names?"

End of story. Conversation over. My father would get up, turn up the TV, and leave the room, questions unanswered.

As I grew older, I would time and again ask my father to tell me what really happened to him during the war. I told him I wanted to memorialize his story, to write a book about it.

"Sure, why not?"

"Okay, when?"

"Any time."

"How about now?"

"Not now."

"When?"

"I don't know."

"Next week?"

"One day we'll do it."

Even if the urgency was lacking, the idea seemed to spark something in him. What was it? A flicker of hope, hope that disclosure would be an unburdening and a catharsis, would make it all good — finally? That was what I hoped. But it never happened. He never opened up to me, at least not when he was alive.

My mother's wartime experiences remained unspoken. But I recall the time we went to visit her in the hospital where she was confined after a gallbladder operation, and I instinctively knew she was at some level reliving her internment. I remember how apprehensive I was, not wanting to see her ill and weak. But she didn't look unwell; in fact, you couldn't tell there was anything wrong with her. She had settled in and was in no great hurry to leave, which surprised me because this wasn't her home and I didn't think she belonged there. We brought her a picnic cooler full of food. She eagerly looked through it, noting the Chelsea buns and Napoleons, the peaches and pears, walnuts, knishes. Instead of offering them to us, she barely thanked us and retreated across the room where a woman, who looked too weak to get out of bed, suddenly came to life when Luba showed her all the goodies, which they proceeded to share like schoolgirls with the latest teen magazine. It surprised me that the woman Luba was sharing with was not Jewish. It contravened everything my parents had taught us, explicitly and implicitly, about the importance of sticking with our own. Our visit ended with Luba sitting on her new friend's bed and chowing down with her. We just kind of faded away.

When my mother was asked about her time in Bergen-Belsen, she was even less forthcoming than my father. She had no living immediate family but every now and then someone she said was a cousin popped up.

"Who is that? Whose child?" I would ask.

No further word about her family would pass her lips. But on Friday evenings when, in the dining room, she would light the Sabbath candles, her hands and eyes betrayed her secrets. Beginning with the three circles she drew above the flickering flames, she would pull the light ineluctably toward her face, almost pleading, toward eyes now flooded with tears, eyes that at this eternal moment divulged the horror and terror of an anguish buried so deep that for only a few seconds every week in the safety of prayer would she allow the images to surface.

I remember watching from the hallway, transfixed in her unremitting present. Gravity has drawn the sleeves of her blouse down to her elbows, her turquoise number now exposed. I don't know what this woman, who has not yet become my mother, sees on the screen of her hands, but I feel its dark heft and dare not ask. It is my mother who lifts cupped hands from her eyes and exhales these final incantatory words, "*Lihadlik ner shel shabat.*" (To kindle the Sabbath candles.)

The meal is about to begin, the silence loud in her; the noise of my brothers colliding at the table, a respite.

4

Enchantments

ALL THROUGH ELEMENTARY SCHOOL, I WAS friends with a pretty brown-haired girl named Sandy Ryan. In the schoolyard on her bike one day, she taught me how to ride, and I clowned around and made her laugh so hard, she peed in her pants. I didn't have my own bike. Abie had his Raleigh but it was used for work not play and he would never let me ride it. Sandy's mother was one of the Inner City Angels who came into the school as a volunteer drama teacher. Her husband's name was Oscar, and why I remember that I don't know. Maybe it was because it sounded so *Father Knows Best*. It was at their apartment that I was first exposed to pussy willows in a vase and enchanting landscapes by the Group of Seven on wall-mounted postcards. I'd never seen such captivating scenes, except one day when I was visiting another school friend who lived six blocks away on Dupont Street. Looking out his kitchen window, I thought I was dreaming. I blinked several times but the vision did not evaporate. In my view was a castle just like in the Red and Blue Fairy tale books I had been devouring, a castle on a hill in the distance but not too distant, a castle they called Casa Loma, a castle that was part of my world.

There were few books in our home, no love shown for the written word, and little appreciation on my part of the barrier to literacy my parents faced with English as a foreign language. Yet stories and storytelling were prized, especially when we went to bed and Abie or Charlie regaled David and me with tales of Moishe Pipik and Rivka the Kishka, or threatened us with the appearance of the Baba Yaga, the legendary monster who loves to eat little children, but only if they are awake. In later years, my mother would catch the bug for reading but her interest would be confined to magazines like *True Confessions* and *Modern Romance*, which she called her "lovebooks," supplements to the TV soap operas she became wired to.

I was a big fan of the nonsense poems of Edward Lear, which I discovered when I volunteered to work in the school library reshelving books. I still remember a silly one in the form of a pompous speech, perhaps a keynote address, that I set down here from memory and never fails to tickle me: "Ladies and Gentlebeans / I come before you / To stand behind you / To tell you something / I know nothing about. / Next Thursday / Which is Good Friday / There will be a mothers' meeting / For fathers only. / Come if you can't / And if you can / Please stay at home …"

My favourite books invariably involved some form of enchantment, especially if the magic went awry as it did in a book called *Half Magic* in which wishes were only half-filled, creating unforeseen havoc for the children who had found a half-assed talisman. Another book that caught my fancy was *Carbonel: The Prince of Cats* about a cat under a witch's spell, and I fantasized having a cat of my own, preferably one, like Carbonel, that could speak.

I did get a cat one day, from where or whom I don't know. It arrived on the scene not long after I witnessed my mother, a frying pan held high, trying to flatten a mouse that had emerged from the drawer at the bottom of the oven, dashed across a stretch of kitchen floor, and disappeared into a crack between the floor and wall. The cat was a fully grown female tabby, browny silver, lumpy, and loving. I named her Matilda. I would feed and brush her, pick her up, carry her about the house, and kiss her on what passed for lips. My mother found it disgusting and unsanitary, and hounded me to nix the kisses. Which I couldn't do. My brothers seemed indifferent to the animal.

One day, a flyer arrived at our house. A pet show was about to be held at the YM-YWHA at Spadina and Bloor, a beauty pageant for cats and dogs! I was beside myself with anticipation, intent upon giving the cat some extra grooming when I got home from school, not that her winning beauty required enhancing. But Matilda was nowhere to be found. I searched the house upstairs and down, then scoured the neighbourhood, without success. Everyone told me not to worry, that cats sometimes leave home and go prowling, but they come back. They didn't tell me this only applies to tomcats.

Countless catless days passed; the day of the show came and went. Matilda never reappeared. It would be fifty years before I learned what happened to Matilda. My father had driven my cat out of town and left her by the side of the road.

* * *

Living in our Palmerston house was like playing musical chairs — only with rooms. I resided in no fewer than five of them. It wasn't just me but the whole family who reshuffled as space became available when lodgers came into their own and left the abode. Who was to take what room was the subject of heated exchange among me and my brothers. Usually, it was Harvey, the youngest, who lost out. Needless to say, we didn't draw straws.

I have already mentioned the dining room, next to the kitchen, that was my parents' bedroom. It was also mine as an infant and, later, when convalescing from childhood illnesses and operations, like having my tonsils removed. As a toddler, I shared the front room on the second floor with my two older brothers, a large room with a bay window and a gas fireplace that didn't work. It was here that I was frightened into sleep in the summer, before the sun had set, with Baba Yaga stories mere moments before the B.Y. made its rounds in search of young children with their eyes still open.

This was when I first started to *shmotchke*; that is, make a clicking sound with my tongue pulling away from my palate, as if I were sucking on a breast. I would do this automatically, reflexively lulling myself to sleep, but only if I were not bombarded with projectiles and "shaddups," which inevitably followed from Abie. Trouble was I had no choice — I couldn't not do it.

I was desperate to have my own space and, for a time, camped out in a long walk-in closet at the top of the stairs, where my mother would keep her clothes and where Abie would sometimes conceal himself, hoping to delay the delivery of a promised beating when "Deddy" returned. There was little *Lebensraum* here, except in the few inches of space underneath the hanging garments. The pungent smell of mothballs was not ideal, nor were the penetrating eyes of fox stoles that still had heads with teeth clutching tails. But here I could be left in peace, have some privacy, gather my thoughts, prepare for adventures, and *shmotchke* if I needed to. I could even hide miniature New Testaments and other treasures. My mother eventually discovered my squat and was not amused. My protests notwithstanding, I was promptly evicted.

After all the third-floor lodgers moved out, Abie and Charlie moved up and remained there for a time until the Deutsches' room on the second floor became available. The two oldest boys then moved down and I moved up. I had not yet turned eight.

The third floor was an atmospheric space of low ceilings and angled dormers. One of the rooms had an east-facing window that opened onto a small section of the roof that was flat. I would often climb out onto it, sit, and watch squirrels and clouds pass by. It was uncomfortable on the gravel surface so, more taken with the romance than the reality, I seldom stayed out long. Inside I would spend hours pretending I was a writer, organizing pens and pencils and playing with the pigeon slots and drawers in the drop front oak desk, and writing up lists of things to do. The other room at the top of the stairs had its own dry kitchen area, a separate narrow space with cupboards but no sink or fridge. Still, it inspired me to take meals in my rooms like a tenant. I would go to the butcher on Bloor Street and buy freshly sliced bologna, borrow from my mother two slices of bread and some mustard, and voilà — I was grown up and independent. A bologna sandwich never tasted so good.

Mina Binsztok, flanked by brother David (*left*) and me, at Abie's Bar Mitzvah, 1959.

Mina's room on the second floor had a hot plate and a kettle that whistled. Mina would sometimes invite me to sit with her, have a glass of tea and a schmooze. This would always begin with the same question, "So, you have a girlfriend?"

I would shake my head and laugh in embarrassment.

"What about that pretty girl you told me about?"

When I mentioned Sandy's name, Mina's eyes would glow with genuine interest.

"Come on, spill the milk."

I admitted that Sandy had invited me to her cottage on Lake Simcoe in the summer.

"Semele," she said, using the affectionate Yiddish form of my name, while poking me in the ribs, "I'm going to need a new dress for the wedding."

Rare was the time Mina wasn't smiling. Not that she wasn't serious, but laughter was her preferred state of being. Maybe that's what drew me to her, along with the bright red lipsticked lips, the flash of gold in her teeth, the sparkle and joie de vivre that belied what then would have been called "spinsterhood." I remember her in a floral print dress, a black cardigan draped over her shoulders, sitting at a card table playing poker with a group of women, including my mother. The women called themselves the Tikvah Club (*tikvah* in Hebrew means hope), and they met every Tuesday evening to play. That Mina had a turquoise tattoo on her forearm was to be expected among the women who held their cards close, rapped their knuckles on the table, and intoned, "Check!"

When I inherited Mina's room, I was in glory land. It was quiet and private yet, as the geographic centre of the house, in the middle of everything. There was nothing special about its size, nor its solitary window overlooking London Street, but its two porcelain sconces with naked light bulbs juxtaposed classic and modern and provided an atmosphere I found transporting. Ghosts inhabited this room, and I don't remember who they were although they seemed to know me, as if they were friends come to visit. Whether they were visions or dreams, it mattered not. In my room, I was never afraid.

On my ninth birthday, my father gave me a Kodak camera, not a Brownie but a newer model with a flash attachment that screwed into its side. As far as I remember, this was the only present he ever gave me when I was a child. Birthdays, except for Bar Mitzvahs, were never acknowledged. I don't know what the deal was with this camera, and even today I can scarcely believe he bought it for me. I think, by chance, someone just happened to give it to him and, luckily, it really was what I wanted.

You had to load the film away from direct light. I remember doing so one day, taking extra precaution not to expose and spoil the old roll. To dim the light, I draped my flannel pyjamas over the sconces, the bottoms on one, the top on the other. A sudden cough made me notice smoke clouding the room. I managed to grab and stomp on my PJs just before they went up in flames. The bottoms were still intact, but I rolled up the seared top and hid it in a garbage bin. Thereafter I would change film in the darkness of a closet, and I made do with a pair of old polo pyjamas.

*   *   *

When Sandy and I were in grade six, her mother directed a production of *Alice in Wonderland* in which I got to play the March Hare. We provided the entertainment for the school's awards assembly. I begged my parents to attend. Unlike my stage debut in grade one as a Litterbug, this time I had speaking lines and floppy ears. Sandy was the Mad Hatter. More importantly, we both won the school's top academic award that year, a Kiwanis Club scholarship, each receiving a cheque for fifteen dollars. Even though a good number of parents were in attendance, including Sandy's, mine were not part of the picture. Nor did they come to see me at Massey Hall when I performed as a soprano in a city-wide choir, having rehearsed for months in the auditorium at Central Tech High School songs like "The Maple Leaf Forever," "Waltzing Matilda," and "Jerusalem." My disappointment in their failure to appear reinforced my aloneness and a sense that nothing I could ever do would be sufficient to gain their attention, if not their approval and love. Little wonder that my teacher made the following comment in my final report card that year: "Sammy has developed a habit of worrying that I don't like to see in someone so young."

When I received an invitation to the Kiwanis Club awards dinner, I didn't bother to tell my parents about it. Sandy was unable to attend, so I ended up going by myself, worried about eating the chicken, using the wrong fork, and smacking my lips. But I had reaped my reward and had to accept the consequences. A kind Kiwanian seated next to me sensed my discomfort.

"Just use your fingers," he said.

The Kiwanis Boys Club in the basement of a church at Lennox and Bathurst Street (now the Randolph Centre for the Arts) became a favourite hangout. To get in, you had to walk down a set of metal fire escape stairs that overlooked a large room with mats and boxing and gymnastic equipment. At the back, there was a smaller room with a tattered couch where I would play trivia with friends, gleaning questions from a book I had discovered in a bookcase under some *Reader's Digests*.

Friday nights, there were dances for the older kids held in the big room. Girls would be invited, too, mostly neighbourhood Brownies or Girl Guides. Being too young, I would have to sneak in or, if caught, use Charlie's ID that I had snatched from his bedside. I loved to dance and, from a young age, was good at it. It didn't bother me that the girls I danced with were older. I was even sought out as a dance partner at weddings and Bar Mitzvahs by relatives and friends of my parents, and we'd whirl around the dance floor like Fred and Ginger.

I used to entertain the adults in my household with a Charlie Chaplin Tramp imitation. I would use a stick for a cane, wear an invisible bowler and moustache, turn my feet out and waddle-walk in our cramped living room, twirling my "cane" to guffaws and knee slapping of my rapt audience.

* * *

Seldom did I do anything with my brothers outside the house. An exception was a yearly mid-November activity that brought us joy and not a little spending money. Charlie was the brains behind the operation, which included a couple of his ne'er-do-well friends, David, and me. David and I were excited to hang out with the older boys and do something special. We would rise long before the sun and assemble in our living room, where we'd find boxes and boxes of balloons and colourful, iridescent-feathered birds, called "birdies," that twirled at the end of a stick. Some two or three gross altogether, these Charlie would purchase in advance at the Balloon King downtown on Bathurst Street near Dundas. Now it was up to us to inflate the balloons as quickly as we could, taking care not to pop them. Using sheer lung power — we had no pumps — did the trick, with the welcome bonus of a head-spinning euphoria. Once inflated and the ends tied off, the balloons would be tied onto long, elastic strings so they could be carried by the handful and bobbed up and down. We were off to sell balloons at the Eaton's annual Santa Claus Parade, the largest in North America in the 1950s, six miles long and hundreds of thousands of spectators.

We'd spread out like the Bowery Boys over a few blocks of the parade route down Yonge Street. It was always cold that day and as much as we would bundle up, we'd be freezing. We needed our hands ungloved to handle the merchandise, take cash, and give change. But the event provided its own kind of heat. We'd walk on the road between the dazzling floats and the spectators gathered on the sidewalks.

"Birdies, birdies, get your birdies here!"

"Balloonies for the kidaroonies!"

Our enthusiasm was infectious, and I recall feeling a kind of performance high, executing my role with total abandon, feeding off the crowd's appreciative, approving energy. Parents were powerless to resist their wide-eyed children, and there was good cheer abounding. As quickly as the balloons were sold, Charlie would be there replenishing our stock. But it was not just a commercial enterprise. We were core participants in a landmark event. It was heartening to see the joy of kids our age and their parents, and to glimpse the parade as it went by. David and I shared in the anticipation of Santa's appearance on the final float, the climax of the parade, by which time all our goods would have been sold, and we could stand by quietly and watch. How wonderful as Jewish boys to be part of this Christian ritual.

After the parade, we would get warm at Bassel's restaurant and feast on square hamburgers, which was like manna to us, a treat because eating in restaurants, given the cost, was not something we ever did. Later, at home, Charlie would proudly collect all the money, subtract his expenses, and divvy up the rest according to plan. He was just happy being there, having organized a successful adventure and sharing it with his younger brothers. I loved the extra money it brought in and, most of all, how it lessened the sting of our separateness — from the dominant culture and from one another.

5

Disenchantments

I WAS EMBARRASSED BY MY PARENTS, THEIR old country ways, their inability to speak English, their loudness, shortness, and general non-Canadian-ness. My mother, who was raven-haired, olive-skinned, and four feet eleven, had a curious habit of sipping tea from a glass while holding a sugar cube between her teeth in the manner of Roma women in old Hollywood movies. I always thought that had a lot of style, but it wasn't one I would necessarily want my friends to see. That my mother became an Avon lady and my father came to be called "Ralph" didn't help. The parents of my friends seemed so much more attractive. The Canadian ones, that is.

My father worked in a tailor shop on Bloor Street near Bay long before it was fashionable. Eventually, he and another Polish survivor, a Galizianer named Benyek Weinstein, opened their own store midtown near Yonge and Eglinton, B&R Custom Tailors. At some point, they had a fight and parted ways. My father bought out Mr. Weinstein, although the *B* in the shop's name never disappeared.

Saturdays when I was eleven or twelve, I used to work at B&R, sweeping up threads, doing bank deposits for my barely literate father, and taking care of other writing chores that came up. My father could only print simple words — words that were often childishly misspelled, and in a lavish European style replete with decorative swirls painstakingly executed with multiple retraced strokes. His penmanship better suited the suit jackets and pants he deftly drew, line sketches tossed off without ornament or self-consciousness. He would ask me to label the drawings with the appropriate information for each customer: slash or straight pockets; whether they dressed to the left or right; their inseam and outside seam lengths; lapel notches, with or without buttonhole; number of vents on the jacket (zero, one, or two); and other such design details.

These tasks were, for me, mindless exercises that soon gave way to boredom. My father would bribe me for my presence with a newspaper bundle of English-style fish and chips from the restaurant down the street or with Wiener schnitzel on a kaiser from the narrow Austrian grill next door. I wanted to learn how to use his sewing machine, how to make things, but he categorically refused to teach me. If it wasn't writing, then it wasn't for me; he didn't want me to work with my hands like him.

I remember how obsequious he was with wealthy customers. Subservient and soft-spoken, a tape measure dangling like a stethoscope around his neck, he would flatten their lapels, give a gentle tug on the hem at the back of their jackets, pick off stray threads or bits of fluff, admire their figures in the three-sided mirror. But when the clients left, the solicitousness left, too, replaced by contempt and curse words — so plentiful in Yiddish! — that littered the shop as profusely as the basting threads scattered on the floor. Later I would hear him bragging to others about having the president of Frigidaire as one of his clients, how they were on a first-name basis. That's how important my father was and how great a tailor. But I knew he didn't believe it.

My father's braggadocio was the same when he spoke of his *lager* experiences. His stories — the few that he told — I didn't believe a word of. Invariably, they involved his getting the best of some Nazi by tricking him into handing over a chocolate bar in exchange for something of little worth like having a button resewn. Rachmil Chaiton, ever the wily, triumphant free agent, not a hint of prisoner about him.

* * *

From time to time, when my father had personal or business matters to attend to, he would take me along for the ride in his 1958 Buick Roadmaster. We would sometimes stop by a two-storey duplex in Forest Hill, just north of Upper Canada College, to visit an old Jewish man who lived alone. I thought this was kind of my dad, trying to allay the old man's loneliness. Compared to us, the man seemed well-to-do. He had a remote control for his TV, something unheard of in those days. Among my brothers and me, deciding who was going to get up off the floor (furniture was not meant to be sat upon by children) and change the channel was the cause of many a fight. We'd have the energy to duke it out but none for taking a few steps to the TV set to twist a dial.

On one of these visits, I went into the bedsitting room to watch TV while my father looked in on the old man, who was upstairs taking a bath. The remote control was a weighty thing with buttons you had to press with all your weight to get their magic to work. Captivated by its high-tech novelty, I quickly became more interested in changing channels and raising and lowering the volume than watching wrestling, bowling, or *Tiny Talent Time*.

"Put that down," said my father on entering the room.

"Why?"

"Leyg es arop!" (Put it down!)

"I'm not doing anything."

"You'll break it. It's not yours."

I set the remote down on the coffee table. My father started rifling through dresser drawers; he found a stash of money and began to stuff his pockets. Hearing a noise, he went out into the hall and looked up the stairs. He quickly came back into the room, helped himself to a few more fistfuls of coin, and closed the drawer.

I guess my father saw the look on my face because he started mumbling, "Why should one man have so much? He's not going to need it, his life is almost over, won't know anything's missing anyway...."

My father lost my respect that day and I was ashamed of being his son. I berated myself for assuming we were visiting this man, who had no family, out of the goodness of my father's heart. I think one of my brothers was with me, probably David, although neither of us said anything at the time nor mentioned the incident any time thereafter.

※ ※ ※

When I was ten, we left downtown for the suburbs. Leaving our Palmerston house marked the beginning of a more unhappy period in my life. We moved to the middle floor of a triplex apartment building that my father, after selling Palmerston, had bought on Wilson Avenue, following the ill-considered lead of B of B&R, who had bought a triplex on the next block. Our apartment, compared to the house, was small, sterile, uninteresting, and held little possibility for adventure. There were no boarders; indeed, no room for anyone outside our nuclear family. This was when a feeling of being trapped first surfaced in me.

I now shared a room with Abie; David and Charlie shared another bedroom. Harvey, the youngest, was as usual on a cot in my parents' bedroom. Abie didn't want to room with any of the others because they were slobs. He was fanatically meticulous about his clothes, which were always impeccably folded or hung in the closet he monopolized. He had an amazing collection of mohair sweaters and wool cardigans, many of which he bought at Studio 267 on Yonge Street. If I touched anything of his, I could lose my life.

My life was threatened often, what with the *shmotch-ke*'ing that did not abate, and my practising the violin, which he smashed over my head when his studying was interrupted one too many times. I don't remember this, and I think Abe's memory stems from a cartoon or Marx Brothers movie. Anyway, he's right that our conflicts didn't stop at threats. The no-holds-barred fights continued throughout my childhood, raging battles in which I didn't shy away from attacking my older brothers if necessary. I knew I'd get beaten, but not before inflicting damage on them. Sometimes at night, I would get struck on the side of my head by a targeted slipper or feel myself being smothered, a pillow held down over my face to get me to shut the fuck up.

I despaired of ever not *shmotchke'*ing, and I panicked about going to summer camp and sharing a cabin with others. I envisioned myself married and having to explain to my wife what that infernal sound was. I don't know what made me stop — maybe it was the potential embarrassment with my peers — but I feel like I could take it up again at any moment. Did my mother breastfeed me too long? I would swear, her full breasts and nipples the size of potato latkes I can still remember, up close.

My father used to come home from work, set his fedora on the highboy in his bedroom, and undress. In boxer shorts, knee socks, and off-white sleeveless undershirt, he'd place his jacket on a hanger in the closet and hang his pants over the knob on the inside of the bedroom door, at the top of which hung a huge calendar from the Workmen's Circle. Still in his underwear, he'd go to the kitchen and take his seat at the end of the Formica table. My mother would set in front of him a special plate, usually with the head of a carp lying sideways, its fish eye staring blankly up at him, not that he noticed. He, too, would sit and stare at nothing, say nothing, slowly picking away at the fish's flesh.

"Mrs. Tannenbaum has a new fur coat."

"Luba, don't bother me. *Lomich esn.*" (Let me eat.)

As tiny fish bones mounded on my father's plate, a sudden thirst would tug at his attention, prompting a thick glass seltzer bottle to appear within arm's reach; it was topped by a metal trigger that looked weathered like a prewar relic and so substantial it could have pumped up the Hindenburg. My father would lean forward, squeeze the trigger by making a fist, fill his glass with effervescing soda water, then chugalug, his pinky lifted to the air as if he were fingering a silver flute. Soon to follow: a burp reverberating like a two-toned *greps*, its Yiddish *mot juste.*

"Dad, I need an increase in my allowance."

"Leave him alone. Can't you see he's eating?"

The breadwinner's meal taken care of, my mother's next chore would be to ascertain what each of her five sons would like in his chicken soup broth.

"Knaydlech? Mandlen? Lokshn?"

Abie would have the matzoh balls, David the soup nuts, Charlie the noodles, and Harvey, whatever was left over. Everyone was catered to à la carte. I wanted none of it, but that was never on the menu. Being a refusenik was my way of rebelling against my controlling Jewish mother, a way perhaps of getting more attention from her by withholding the very thing she seemed to cherish most — my appetite.

"Semele, would you like tomato soup from a can?"

"I'm not hungry."

"You have to eat something."

"I don't want soup."

"Then I'll make you French toast, just the way you like it."

"I'm not hungry."

This was when I'd get up and head into my parents' bedroom, careful not to snag my father's laden trousers while closing the door behind me. David and I, separately and individually, developed a habit of helping ourselves to bills from the wallet in his right back pocket and to loose change in the front left. This, we'd reassure ourselves, was because our allowance was insufficient to meet our needs. Retrospection tells a different story. Regardless, I don't know if my father ever had the remotest idea.

* * *

Turning thirteen, I thought I'd give the Judaism thing a whirl. All my male friends were having Bar Mitzvahs and, in my family, it was a given that I would, too. Like my older brothers before me, I diligently studied my portion of the Torah. But I took it even further. I began to don tefillin first thing in the morning, wrapping leather thongs around forehead and left arm, then praying. Oh yes, I was going to be a good Jew.

I was Bar Mitzvah'd in the Viewmount Shul, an orthodox synagogue on Bathurst Street that was attended by my mother's cousin, my godfather, Abraham Bleeman, who we called Avrum. Avrum Bleeman was a man of extreme wealth and Jewish orthodoxy to match. I was persuaded to spend the night before my Bar Mitzvah at his house so that I could walk to the synagogue and not have to contravene Sabbath rules by riding in a car. It didn't seem to matter that my parents and brothers were driving to the shul and would be going to hell in a handbasket.

Left: My mother and father draping me with a tallis at my Bar Mitzvah, 1963. *Right, from the left*: Cousins Alf and Howard Chaiton and their parents — my Auntie Sallah and Uncle Yankel — and me, the Bar Mitzvah boy.

As a Bar Mitzvah gift, Avrum gave me a three-volume set of books, *The Code of Jewish Law*. There were rules governing everything. I skimmed the books for the juicy parts and found a section on masturbation and other forbidden pleasures. That was the first sour note in my conversion. Spilling your seed on the earth was a definite no-no, but, as I didn't think Kleenex counted as earth, I carried on. I was edified to learn that a good Jew must do his duty before God and copulate with his wife every Friday evening after the sun goes down. This part sounded doable but when it was coupled with the injunction for a good Jew to have zillions of children, I got really turned off. I never fantasized about having my own children. I never wanted to bring more hapless souls into the sorrow of this world — especially ones that sprang from my lineage.

A sit-down dinner with three hundred and fifty of my parents' closest friends on November 10, 1963, a Sunday, at a banquet hall on Steeles Avenue. No hall of suitable capacity was available closer to my actual October birthday. The size of my parents' social network was astounding. There were the *kortnshpielers* (the card players); the people in the *shmateh* business, the garment factory owners and workers, the furriers, the pressers, the finishers; the shoemakers; the jewellers; the builders; those who summered in Crystal Beach and Jackson's Point, who sent their kids to Camp Northland and Camp B'nai Brith, who attended various synagogues along the Bathurst Street corridor and spent their winters in Miami Beach. Survivors all, their lives an endless round of poker games and *simchas*. Almost every Sunday, there'd be a bris or Bar Mitzvah or wedding to attend. They would greet one another with "*Oyf simchas!*" (May we meet only on celebrations!) I would ask my parents who their friends were, where and how they met, how long they had known them. *"Zey zaynen landsmen"* was the usual reply. No defining details of time or place or the particulars of their relationship were forthcoming. No context. "From the old country" was about it.

Except for a few relatives and friends, I didn't know most of the people at the event held supposedly in my honour, and they didn't know me. They would approach, shake my hand with a hearty *"Mazel tov!"* and present me a sealed envelope with cash or a cheque. Some gave their envelopes to one of my brothers or friends, thinking they were me. The envelopes eventually made their way into the cummerbund of the rented tuxedo I wore, and the haul was counted later that night by Charlie. It added up to over three thousand dollars, which was sufficient to cover the cost of the celebration — and that's what it went for. Other than the three-volume *Code of Jewish Law*, there wasn't anything else I got to keep.

Not much stands out for me about that night of my celebration. It was Abie's first date with Sue, who went on to be his wife and the mother of his first two children. I remember her standing in the doorway to the hall in an orange satin knee-length dress with matching satin-covered pumps, clutching her clutch. My mother, too, carried a clutch and wore satin pumps that matched her fitted, floor-length, custom-made gown. She also adorned herself with pearls around her neck and in her hair, and long, white evening gloves à la Jackie Kennedy. My parents spared no expense putting on a show trumpeting their success at our family's affairs. Over the years, as the family's prosperity increased, Mom's *simcha* gowns became progressively more resplendent, with hand-sewn beads, high Elizabethan collars, and tiaras. My father would tailor himself a new tuxedo for each new celebration, but his style never changed.

My parents, happier than I've ever seen them, prepare to
dance at Abie's Bar Mitzvah, 1959.

My devotion to Judaism was short-lived. Less than two weeks after my Bar Mitzvah, we were learning about South African apartheid when our grade eight geography class was interrupted. Our teacher, Miss Thompson, got called out to the hall. She returned a few minutes later, looking paler than usual. She announced that classes were suspended, and we were being sent home early. She paused for a moment, inhaled, and said, "The American president has been shot."

I didn't think that if there was a God, this kind of behaviour would be allowed. I had thought my Uncle Yankel looked like JFK. Now that JFK had been shot, what would that portend for Yankel? It felt weird, leaving the school in the early afternoon, like a continuation of the Cuban Missile Crisis when I wandered around my neighbourhood hearing air raid sirens and looking up at the sky for a sign of the doom that had already invaded my ears and gut. No one was visible on the streets, not even a passing car. It seemed pointless to hide. Where would I go?

When I got home that late November day, I was afraid. None of my brothers was home. I found my mother frozen on a loveseat in front of the TV set, her mind somewhere else.

"Oy gevald, gevald!"

Save for these few words, she didn't speak. Her silence was supplanted by the frenzy of nonstop TV coverage.

"Mom, Mom?"

Her demeanour freaked me out even more than the news of President Kennedy's shooting. I was at a loss as to how to draw her out of this paralysis. I touched her arm and she recoiled.

"Mom, it's going to be okay."

I didn't really believe what I was saying. I was trying to soothe my mother but couldn't even begin to reach her. I needed to do something, so I called my best friend.

"Hi, Alan. Isn't *From Russia with Love* playing tonight?"

It was a Friday, and in those days, we went to the movies every Friday evening. I longed for everything to be normal. So, as if nothing unusual was happening, Alan and I went to see the James Bond movie that had just opened. It was a perfect fantasy for that night, but by the time we emerged from the darkness of the cinema to the jarring, artificial lights of the evening, President Kennedy had been confirmed undeniably dead, and the sound of life had resumed in our home.

Two days later cause was found for further "*oy gevalds.*"

My mother and I were watching TV; I can't remember what, but it wasn't *I Love Lucy*, which we used to relish together, my enjoyment stemming mostly from her uncontrollable laughter. The program was interrupted by live coverage of the news. We watched as Lee Harvey Oswald, escorted in police custody through the basement of the Dallas Police Headquarters, was suddenly shot and killed by Jack Ruby, who I later found out was the son of Polish Orthodox Jews. Just as suddenly, Luba unstuck herself from the plastic on the loveseat, got up, and left the room. I imagined it was to pack up the crystal, get ready to flee. That she no longer felt safe here made me feel vulnerable, too. I wanted to shout down the hall and tell her not to forget the Dresden figurine but I was paralyzed with fear, and the words would not come.

* * *

I never went to the movies with my mother, let alone with Mina, but one day I did. I was fifteen and it was a Polish film called *The Shop on Main Street* starring Ida Kaminska, an actress well known to my companions. I didn't know what to expect. Suddenly, I found myself in the middle of a Holocaust movie, Ida playing an elderly Jewish widow who is dispossessed of her sewing goods store but doesn't realize it. Not long into the film, I noticed Mommy and Mina quietly sobbing. I was unnerved, didn't know what to say, what to do. What made me come to see this? Luba and Mina continued whispering to each other in Polish. I didn't know what memories they were sharing, but I started weeping, too. The film went on to win the Academy Award in 1966 for Best Foreign Language Film.

* * *

In Ashkenazi Jewish culture, you can't be named after a relative who is still alive, so names like Thurston Howell III are non-starters. I don't know what dead relative I was named after. My Hebrew name is Shlomo, which is King Solomon's name. In Yiddish, I was often called "Semele" or "Semenu," a diminutive form, like Sammy, which was my name until junior high school, and continued to be used by Mother, long after I had grown up. My mother also called me the "*Grineh Yazus*," or the "Green Jesus," on account of my olive skin and long curly hair. "Tula" was another I liked the affectionate sound of, with its "oo" and "ah," soft "t," and liquid "l." I asked my mother where the name came from.

"Tula was our village idiot."

I love the sound of words, particularly names. I joke about having a mild case of Tourette's, and my friends always bring me names they think I might like, like Shoshana Zuboff. No name could top one of the witnesses in the O.J. Simpson trial, Sukru Boztepe, which sounds like "Sue Crew Bosteppie," and I can repeat it endlessly with great delight on my tongue.

My Uncle Jacob had a superb name. In Yiddish it was Yankel but we called him Uncle Yunkel. Uncle Yunkel (sorry, I just had to repeat it) was my father's youngest brother. I thought Uncle Yunkel (ditto) was very handsome. I picture him smoking and extinguishing his cigarette on a round metal ashtray, always close by, with a knob you pressed to make the butts disappear into its receptacle down below. After he and his family moved from Euclid Avenue, they lived for a while in a house on Boon Avenue near St. Clair and Dufferin, then moved on up to a small bungalow on Invermay, in the Bathurst-Wilson area. His claim to fame was an injury sustained when a small Canadian Forces plane crashed into his backyard. The four military men onboard lost their lives on impact. Upon hearing the crash, my uncle ran out of the house, taking my Aunt Sallah and cousins Howard and Gail to safety. He ran back into the house to look for Alf, slipped on the threshold, and cracked two ribs. If this wasn't the most heroic of injuries, he still had some connection to greatness. It was a Friday, and the story was on the front page of all the Saturday local newspapers. For years I proudly kept the February 3, 1968, copy of the *Toronto Star*. I scarcely noticed that the papers played up the terror of a Holocaust survivor, flashing back to aerial bombardments in the war and panicking, thinking it had all started again. The widows of the crash victims befriended my aunt and uncle and, for years afterwards, exchanged Christmas cards with them.

As I mentioned, accidents featured prominently in my childhood. The most upsetting happened one night when my brothers and I were already in bed. My parents had gone to a *simcha*, a Bar Mitzvah or a wedding. When the phone rang and woke us up, I assumed they were already home, it being after midnight. Abie answered. It was my mother calling from the hospital. She and my father had been in a car accident — they had smashed into a brick wall.

Abie nonchalantly put the phone down and went back to bed.

"Well, what happened?"

"I don't know."

"Was Mommy trying to drive? She doesn't even have her licence yet!"

"I don't know."

"Are they all right? Are they coming home?"

"I guess so."

None of my brothers seemed to be concerned. Everyone went back to bed, as if sleeping were more important than talking and worrying together. I couldn't believe it. Life goes on no matter who falls by the wayside, even if it's our parents? Was that a lesson we'd learned growing up in our household?

It was like what happened at Charlie's Bar Mitzvah reception. I was dancing with Mina, spinning her around the hall in a spirited and lively polka. Suddenly a man, who had also been dancing, fell down. His face had turned greeny-grey and he lay lifeless on the floor. Someone said he was a distant relation of my mother's. Mina's reaction surprised me. She wanted to keep dancing and seemed more upset that our dance was interrupted than that the man had died. I didn't consider then that something in Mina's personal history may have inured her to death. Later I tried to make sense of the incident. Charlie becomes a man and a relative becomes no-longer-a-man, a lesson on the circularity and balance of life? It was hard not to think this did not augur well for Charlie's incipient adulthood.

Regarding his Bar Mitzvah, David was to have his own kind of portent. He was always the contrary one, a little chubby and cantankerous, would go out of his way to cause everyone grief, like making bulldog faces to deliberately ruin family photos. When he wanted to get back at me, David was not above ratting me out for smoking cigarettes. My parents never had time for him, nor interest in anything that interested him. A quick and brilliant mind, he loved to take things apart and put them back together. I remember one of his school projects, an impressive towerlike structure he built of popsicle sticks held together by Elmer's Glue. He begged my parents for money to buy more supplies to finish the building.

"You call that a building?"

They refused, and David refused to study for his Bar Mitzvah, missing lesson after lesson. My father threatened, "Fine, then you won't have a Bar Mitzvah."

And David retorted, "I don't care. Who needs it? It's only for your fucking friends anyway."

My mother tried coaxing him to study, but to no avail. He alone of all the boys never had a Bar Mitzvah and grew up never forgiving my parents for it. They made sure, however, that a photo was taken with him wearing a yarmulke and with a tallis around his shoulders, as if this were his Bar Mitzvah photo. None of my parents' poker-playing buddies were the wiser. It was displayed on the wall in the dining room alongside the studio Bar Mitzvah portraits of the other four boys, authentication of "becoming a man" in the Chaiton household.

6

Meshuga

SKINNY JEANS, PENNY LOAFERS, MADRAS shirts, and fixed noses — that was the style among my peers in the early sixties. Having my nose fixed was never an option because my parents couldn't afford it. Not that I seriously wanted to. I couldn't imagine not having the large nose that I inherited from my father. To change what I considered an integral part of my character, as a route toward self-improvement, would smack too overtly of self-hatred. Yet the kids of rich Jews that I knew got their noses fixed with the insouciance of a teen getting a tattoo today. I guess they didn't heed comedian David Steinberg's warning: When you have your own child, it's going to come out with a big schnoz, and that is God's way of going, "Booga, Booga!" You can run but you can't hide. Nothing disappears.

There were often dances, sock hops or socials, on Saturday nights at the YM-YWHA on Bathurst Street north of Sheppard Avenue. My childhood love for dancing had not abated, and I was getting into funky American soul music like "Harlem Shuffle" by Bob & Earl. I eschewed the Swim and the Fish for the Boogaloo and the Skate, and there were always attractive young women eager to share the dance floor with me. An added bonus: I didn't have to talk while fast dancing. I could be gliding, slipping, dipping, and turning, smoothly and wordlessly.

One evening, a young woman named Sonia, in a tight-fitting one-shoulder leopard print dress, caught my eye. She accepted my invitation to dance. "Shotgun" by Jr. Walker and the All Stars launched us into a funky groove; "The Jerk" by the Larks and Wilson Pickett's "In the Midnight Hour" kept it going. When the music slowed with "Unchained Melody" by the Righteous Brothers, "Yes, I'm Ready" by Barbara Mason, and Solomon Burke's "Tonight's the Night," I was happy to get close, slow dancing cheek to cheek. I could have danced all night, but Sonia whispered she had to leave early. I asked if I could walk her home and she said yes.

She lived in a high-rise on Bathurst Street near Sheppard. It was a slow stroll up the steep hill to her place. When we arrived at her building, she asked me if I wanted to see the view from the roof. We took the elevator up. It was a warm summer night, and a sultry breeze fanned the rooftop. Not another soul was there. Garish lights leaching up from Sheppard Plaza muted the stars in the night sky, but I didn't care. I put my arm around Sonia and noticed for the first time how petite she was. She nestled snugly into me, and we stared out into space, the wind licking our faces, her hair blowing into her eyes, she tucking the strands behind her earringed ears, to no avail. I had never been with a woman before, not in this way. I made out with several girls but it was little more than necking. Sonia was more of a woman than a girl. I pulled her closer. She turned toward me. We kissed, long and slow.

"I better go."

"Not yet."

"I got to go. I promised my dad I'd be home by eleven."

I tried kissing her again. She pulled away.

"I'll see you at the next dance, if I can."

That was it. She left me standing on the roof, solitary against the night sky.

I took the elevator down, exited into the street, and waited at the red light. I thought of Romeo's line to Juliet, when she booted him out of her room, their first time together, "Wilt thou leave me so unsatisfied?" Juliet's retort must have been on my mind. I crossed the road, stuck out my thumb, trying to hitchhike a ride south. A little white Triumph Spitfire, a two-seater sports car, pulled up.

"Where you going?"

"Wilson Avenue?"

"Okay. Hop in."

The car was cool but the driver looked kind of nerdy, like Truman Capote with thick-rimmed black plastic glasses. I was sullen, quiet. When we reached Wilson Avenue, he offered to drive me all the way home.

"Turn right here."

We got to the strip plaza a block from where I lived and I told him he could let me off. I thanked him for the ride, jumped out of the car, and started walking. He turned the car around, drove back up to me, and rolled the window down.

"Hey, can I ask you something?"

"Sure."

"Well, I was wondering if you were interested in the gay life."

"Excuse me?"

"Are you interested in the gay life?"

I thought about it for a minute. "Gay" was a word for me and most people at that time that only meant happy.

"Yeah, I like to have a good time."

"Do you want me to suck you off?"

"Oh…. Uh…. Okay."

I got back in the car. We drove along Wilson, my heart racing. I questioned what I'd gotten myself into. I had surprised myself and was scared. But the roller coaster had left the station and begun its ascent. When we turned left at Bathurst Street, I realized we were heading back to where we'd started. When we reached the Y, it was now closed. It had a large parking lot down a hill, semi-secluded near a ravine and that's where he parked. He turned to me, reached over the stick shift, and undid the zipper in my pants. He pulled out my boner, bent over, and placed it in his mouth. He started sucking, creating what felt like a moist vacuum. When I started to come, he sucked even harder, faster.

"Ah, ah, ah, ah!!" I cried out, hovering on the border of pleasure and pain.

He kept going, sucking and swallowing like someone starving suddenly fed. I could not believe it, that he was doing this, that I had let him. He asked me if I wanted to do it to him and I declined. He finished himself off in about five seconds in his handkerchief. He asked me if I do any of the lifestyle things, like nude sunbathing.

"No."

"You should try it sometime. Nothing like feeling the hot sun all over your naked body."

He dropped me off at the same spot. I was careful he didn't see which direction I walked so he wouldn't know where I lived. When I got home, I took a shower but couldn't clean off how dirty I felt. I was fourteen years old and had just had my first sexual experience. It had started with a woman and finished with a man.

* * *

I spent grades ten and eleven in torment, and my marks suffered along with me. I had done something disgusting and felt responsible. I had brought this upon myself. I was the one who was hitchhiking. I was the one who had said yes. On the sly, I sought out books about homosexuality. I quickly confirmed that same-sex sex was against the law and considered a mental disorder that required treatment by aversion therapy.

Who could I turn to for support? I was too ashamed to mention it to my brothers. I wouldn't think of opening up to my parents, fearing that not only would they be ashamed of me and angry, but they wouldn't have a clue what to do. Hit me? I was too grown to be strapped. Deny this happened? I tried that but to no avail. Omnipresent Capotes were constant reminders of what I'd done. Everywhere I went, I'd see someone that looked like the bespectacled guy in the Spitfire. I was afraid he was stalking me and that if he caught up with me again, he'd reveal to the world I was a freak who had allowed him to suck my dick.

If I experienced sexual pleasure with a man, then I had to be homosexual. But what about my attraction to women? Was this an either/or situation? Did I have a choice? Or had I crossed a line that could never be uncrossed? I had wanted to live a life that my parents would understand and approve of. I decided to keep silent, and entertained thoughts of suicide, should my anguish become unbearable.

I arrived in grade twelve sexually confused and tied in knots. I also had to make a final decision about my future. I had to choose between studying language and literature in grade thirteen or maths and sciences, which was what I needed to get into medical school. For my parents, the latter was the only course available to me, and especially because my grades were high. But like my brother Abie, I couldn't stand the sight of blood. I nearly passed out when I got a needle. Just the thought of cutting skin with a scalpel would send shivers down my spine and set my whole body trembling. But I couldn't sit down with my parents and reason it out. Conversations were snatched on the fly.

One day, my mother was about to lug a basket of dirty clothes downstairs to the laundry room on the bottom floor of the triplex. She was furious at me for contemplating not taking maths and sciences, a prerequisite to becoming a doctor. I was trying to reason with her, saying I wasn't cut out for medicine, that I loved language and literature. I offered to carry the load downstairs. She ignored me. Halfway down, she stopped, turned, and pinpointed me with coal black eyes.

"Hitler couldn't kill me, but you could."

"What! How can you say that?"

I followed her into the laundry room.

"How can you say that?"

"Pass me the bleach."

Another time I pleaded with my father. "I don't want to be a doctor. I'll become a professor of literature. What's wrong with that?"

"That's not a profession."

I might as well have said that I planned to become a homeless junkie. It's hard not to do what a Holocaust survivor wants you to. Doubly hard when there's two of them and two number tattoos staring you in the face. But it felt so wrong for me.

My paralysis was overcome by counselling from an understanding academic adviser in the Office of Admissions at the University of Toronto. As we spoke of my dilemma, it became clear how much I loved the arts and not the sciences. I decided that my parents' insistence on doctorhood was a Jewish joke that the cosmos was playing on me. When I announced my decision, I made my mother cry and her tears scorched me with their heat. I hated myself for being so cruel. This double bind again led me to think, like the adolescent I was, that death was the only answer.

By this time, Abie had moved out of Wilson Avenue, was married and living downtown with Sue. The room we shared on Wilson Avenue was now all mine. I proceeded to decorate it with pictures of Renaissance, Baroque, and Romantic art I cut out of magazines like *Time* and *Life*. The pictures weren't displayed on the walls but curated according to theme and artfully placed flat on top of dressers in opposite corners of the room. There were only two themes: good and evil, each with its own dedicated corner. I started pacing — not a huge outlet for my pent-up energy, given the room's small size. If I felt one way, I would hang out in that corner; feeling inapposite, I would relocate to the opposite. In the evil corner, there was, for example, Hieronymus Bosch's *Garden of Earthly Delights* for times when I felt overwhelmed by my desires.

This was not a static state of decoration, but a process I began the day before I tried to kill myself. I was like God dividing the waters, separating the land from the sea. The process, not the resulting look, was paramount — the cutting out of pictures, their categorization and placement in the appropriate corner. It wasn't a collage, but a portrait of how I perceived myself at the time, with conflicting impulses that could not be reconciled, but which I attempted to resolve, however instinctively, by division and separation, using art as a vehicle. I was rent in twain, and never the twain did meet.

There was a third corner, too, that contained elements of both, a synthesis I carefully avoided, it being a muddier place to be. I was either wholly holy or decidedly abject. Like William Blake, I was singing songs of innocence or experience and none other.

Yet Botticelli's *Birth of Venus*, which I placed in the white corner, was now found full of ambiguity. I had to move it to the dark side. I needed to take refuge in the prelapsarian garden of Eden. I cut the left panel out of the Bosch triptych and placed it in the arena of innocence.

This was not decoration. It was my suicide note, as close as I could come to articulating my pain. And I knew, as I popped a half bottle's worth of Valium, anyone who found me would not even notice the pictures, let alone decipher their meticulous arrangement.

* * *

Abie was there when I came to. He drove me to Branson Hospital on Finch Avenue. In the Emergency Department, I was still kind of out of it, feeling very stoned and moving in slow motion. My brother spoke to the intake person, and we were asked to wait in a curtained-off area. A nurse came in to take my vitals but before proceeding, she tried to get the facts from me. And I was not too clear. She rolled her eyes.

"Couldn't you have found an easier way to get high?"

"What?"

She moved closer to me to shine a light into my eyes.

"That's what you kids are into these days, isn't it?"

"Fuck off! I'm outta here. Abie, let's go."

So we left.

I told Abie I wasn't ready to go back home. He asked me if I'd like to stay with him and Sue, in their flat on Admiral Road.

"That would be good, but it's kinda far from school."

"Don't worry about school. You just need to get your head together."

My stay at Abie and Sue's turned into a period of non-stop creativity when I spewed out poem after poem, not great works but intense and pregnant with angst and meaning, some of which, despite their fragmentary quality, would be published in my high school yearbook, thanks to its perspicacious literary editor: me. A wonderful poem by Raffi Cavoukian (later, Raffi, the author and singer-songwriter of "Baby Beluga" fame), a riff on Andrew Marvell's "To His Coy Mistress," also made the grade. A poem I wrote later in the year, revealing as much of my literary studies as my state of mind, I set down here from memory:

> You're a Hamlet Dive-in the big city Comedy
> of demon emotions and fears
> tears of alienation, strange sublimation
> of rib-caged body evil into a
> dripping sop drivel
> Up-shrivel down sadness

Ha!
Photograph that laugh and bear it
framed under glass stained
You're not an ass who shits cry,
Stub-born unlife when will you ticket die?
Fee, fie, foe on Tom Fumb's fucking folly
Gib de baby a loli
pop,
Fop, in vain you insane
feign
sanity.

Abie hooked me up with a psychiatrist, a Freudian who sat behind a desk and rarely spoke. Using a tiny metal scraping spoon, he would dig deep into his pipe bowl, bang it on the edge of an earthenware ashtray, scoop from a pouch some aromatic tobacco, tamp it down, slide the pipestem between his teeth, pick up and flick his flint lighter twice, suck hard until the bowl flamed amber and, in the glow of victory, insouciantly lean back in his swivel chair, eyes dreamily directed at the ceiling. Aside from the ritual pipe clatter, not a few of my fifty-minute sessions were spent in silence. If I wasn't feeling suicidal, then I had nothing to talk about, or so I felt. The psychiatrist didn't prod me, but I kept returning for our weekly appointments anyway. These gave my life some regularity and a sense that I was worth fifty minutes of someone else's time, even if his pipe proved more absorbing. I have to say, as inadequate as they were, the sessions helped me get through a precarious period.

After a few weeks living downtown, I moved back home to carry on with school. I hadn't spoken to my parents, nor had they tried to contact me since my suicide attempt. My mother would likely have claimed it was just an accident. I continued to see the psychiatrist. On one occasion, my father picked me up after a session. I got in the car and, instead of the usual silence, he had a question for me.

"*Nu*, are you still crazy?"

"I don't know. Are you?"

The exchange enraged me and solidified my hatred for this man who was utterly lacking in compassion and understanding.

Why couldn't my father speak to me like a mensch? I couldn't say shit to him because he was never honest and open with me. I thought, if only he could reveal his hidden life, his personal history, that would give us some basis for relating. Why wouldn't or couldn't he talk? How often have I tried to answer that question? My answers were always in the form of questions. Was his shame so great that he couldn't admit to his sons what had happened to him? Was he afraid no one would understand? Did he think he'd be tainting this new land, new language, new life with old baggage that didn't belong here? Did he want to protect his children from such ugliness and horror — not give them fodder for nightmares? Did he even have nightmares? Maybe he felt if he began to speak, the floodgates would open and he would break down in tears, never to recover and carry on. But I never saw him cry, never saw him shed even a single tear. Ever. Maybe that's why.

I was unaware of all the emotions that were roiling then in my household, which would become clear to me only much later. All I knew was that I couldn't wait to finish grade thirteen. Getting a high school diploma was not the goal but moving out was. I was dying to get away from my parents, from the suburban desolation of Bathurst-Wilson, and into a community of like-minded people. I was dying to live.

7

Higher Education

AS SOON AS JUNE ROLLED AROUND, I MOVED
out and finally felt free. My life burst with possibility like pent
peony buds after a late spring rain. I was open to experimentation, eager to absorb new ideas and experiences, to participate
in the sixties' counterculture and the social revolution that was
thrillingly under way. I wanted to discover who this person was
who finally felt free.

With an average over 80 percent, I was awarded a four-
hundred-dollar Ontario Scholarship as well as a $150 scholar-
ship to attend University College at the University of Toronto.
It being 1968, that completely covered my tuition. Added to
that, a student loan — then a combination of loan and a bur-
sary that you didn't have to repay — and I was set, my text-
books and living expenses also taken care of.

I went to a poetry reading in a raccoon hideaway, a garage off Admiral Road. I climbed the nearly vertical wood steps, more like a ladder than a staircase, up to the loft. Judith Merril, the science fiction writer with a passion for poetry, bade me welcome. In the flickering candlelight, I discerned a small group of participants. I found an opening in the circle and sat down cross-legged on the wood floor. The rustle of wind through the trees, the chirp of crickets, the evening air intense with the scent of lilac — I was transported. Judith invited us to recite or read anything we wanted to. I intended to read from T.S. Eliot's play *Murder in the Cathedral*. I had been fixated on the Chorus's repeated refrain, "Living and partly living" — my stock answer to anyone who asked how I was doing. When the candle talking-stick arrived in front of me, I changed my plan. I read instead Dylan Thomas's poem "Fern Hill," about loss of innocence and youth and our inattention to the inexorable passage of time:

> Nothing I cared, in the lamb white days, that
>   time would take me
> Up to the swallow thronged loft by the
>   shadow of my hand,
> In the moon that is always rising, …

My reading was received with nods and quiet affirmation. I was thrilled.

I found a flat on Huron Street in the Annex not far from the poetry loft. I was going to share it with Mark Lam, a hip guy I'd met through Irma, an Afghan-coat–wearing chick who was Gilda's best friend. Gilda was someone I was close to. We'd come to know each other as teenagers at a Jewish summer camp in Haliburton, where I worked as a waiter, she as a counsellor.

We read the same books and discussed them, like *Siddhartha* by Hermann Hesse and Sartre's *Nausea*, as well as poetry by Irving Layton and Marianne Moore, in the rec room of her parents' basement while listening to Richie Havens or Laura Nyro. Gilda turned me on to Leonard Cohen's *Beautiful Losers* and to the artists at The Three Schools, like Dennis Burton, who she babysat for. Although Gilda's parents were born in Canada, the Holocaust seemed to have made a bigger mark on her than me. She confided in me of frequent nightmares of being interned, starved, and tortured.

The Huron Street flat was on the second floor of a house within walking distance of the university. It was here that I started smoking dope in earnest and ingesting psychedelics. The living situation was chaotic and I thrived on it, at least initially. Hip people hung out at all hours. Mark had friends who were artists and musicians, like Tony Kosinec (who went on to co-write the "Okay, Blue Jays" baseball ditty), but I wasn't sure how most of the people came to be there, not that I really cared. Those were heady days, heads just drifting in and out. Chris, an English chap, turned me on to *Sgt. Pepper's Lonely Hearts Club Band* by getting me to listen to it high and with a great set of stereo headphones. Another guy, David Cohen, impressed me as a man of the world, always talking about his travels across North Africa, dope he smoked, women he fucked, books like *The Alexandria Quartet* by Lawrence Durrell, and stimulating articles he'd read in *Playboy* and *Esquire*. A head named Rob wore John Lennon wire rims, had hung out with Janis Joplin in Texas and San Francisco and called her "Momma." Gilda's friend, Jules, was a stoner from Montreal whose eyes flashed with wild intelligence. There was Jennifer, a funky chick with funky red hair, who loved to chill, smoke, and laugh. She had a beautiful smile and a businessman brother who, the first time I met him, blew my mind when he fervently argued it was more important to fund the space program than it was to feed poor people.

There was a second Rob. This one always wore a long, chestnut-coloured leather coat over bell bottom blue jeans and Chelsea boots. He had a girlfriend named Jeannie who was Leonard Cohen's cousin. I was loving the freedom of my life, the feeling of connection to great artists, to what was hip and happening in the world. Rob, Jeannie, and I often tripped together. One Saturday, we dropped some acid. I wrote a poem that began "welcome to the land of no superlatives," a place where everything was equally wondrous with no distinction between art and shit. I walked by a mirror. Didn't recognize that the person staring back at me was me, although he looked somewhat familiar and was wearing my favourite acid green turtleneck. I went out for some fresh air and stood on a deck off the second floor at the back of the house. I began to sway in the soft summer air. Moving yet rooted, I was the breeze. I felt the flow up my torso, through my arms, and out through my fingertips. The top of my head opened to the night sky. I beamed beatifically at the moon, convinced I'd reached nirvana and there was nothing left to do but be.

All this came crashing down; the catalyst was a visit. It was a Sunday morning, the doorbell rang, and I went to answer. Standing at the bottom of the steep set of stairs leading to our second-floor flat were my parents. My mother was holding a knotted bow of white string tied around a white bakery box.

"What are you doing here?"

"What do you mean what are we doing here? We've come for a visit."

"Couldn't you have called?"

"We're your parents, we have to call?"

The place was still littered with friends, male and female, who had dropped acid the night before.

"Well, you can't come up. It's not a great time."

My father turned away in disgust.

"Come, Luba. Let's go."

Luba started to leave too, then swung back around. She proffered the white box.

"These are for you."

Reluctantly, I descended the stairs and took the gift.

"Blueberry buns. Your favourite."

A guilt knife to the gut. Ouch. I'd already been feeling shitty, out of control. Didn't know how hard it would be to share a living space with non-family, i.e., with no mother around. Why didn't anyone clean up after themselves, wash the dishes, or sweep the floor? Having a linear conversation seemed impossible; you could start at A but getting to B was a mother. There was no quiet time to read or think. I knew that once classes began, I was going to be in trouble. Mark and I as flatmates barely lasted the summer.

David Cohen was still living with his parents in a swanky apartment not far away. He told me they had a room at the end of a twenty-foot-long hallway that used to be for the help. It had its own bathroom. He said they were looking to rent it out. That was where I moved next.

The building, a dark brick low-rise, had a tiny, elegant European-style elevator with a black grille you had to manually open and close. The entrance floors were comprised of alternating black and white marble squares set in a diamond pattern, and the carpeting on the stairs was plush and red. The Cohens' apartment was on the top floor. It had hardwood floors, elaborate mouldings, and high ceilings. I was living out a fantasy. David's parents, unlike mine, were cosmopolitan and well-educated. David's mother was a social worker and his father, a chemistry professor and researcher at the University of Toronto. He had Parkinson's, shuffled like the *Addams Family*'s Cousin Lurch, had difficulty speaking, and everyone carried on as if he were perfectly normal. He went to work every day according to routine. I felt safe and at home. I had my own space, could read and study in quiet, all within the confines of a family home that appealed to my imagination.

And then there was dance. As I grew up, dancing and my deepest self seemed always in sync. Rhythms coursed with ease through my body, and I loved to move; indeed, I had to move, especially when feeling trapped. It was as if the unhappiness and double binds that I could not put into words were able to find their resolution in my hands, feet, the top of my head, my ears, knees, elbows, spine. And dancing with a partner allowed me to extend comfortably beyond myself, to feel a powerful connection through movement, to converse without having to speak, to feel close and untangled. Dance, for me, was purgation and jubilation, permission to be present, no worries.

How to pursue this joy with intention? I asked Rhonda Ryman, a redhead in my final high school year's English class, for the best place to take dance classes in Toronto. Rhonda had studied ballet and was to become a dance historian and world-renowned expert in the Laban method of dance notation. She suggested that, given my age, modern dance probably would be better for me than ballet since the training was still rigorous but didn't require starting so young. She recommended the Toronto Dance Theatre (TDT) in Yorkville.

The TDT studio was situated at 22 Cumberland Street (before the Pilot Tavern moved in), in a building that looked like a garage, squat and unimposing. With some apprehension, I ascended the narrow staircase to the second floor. A small reception area bustled with people in leotards and knit pants or leg warmers over tights. Live piano music percolated in the background.

Already wearing suitable loose clothing, I registered for the beginners' class and entered the studio. It was a square, fair-sized room with a baby grand piano in the corner, black linoleum floor, and large multipaned warehouse windows facing south over Cumberland. A guy with long hair remained on the floor, stretching after his class. His muscular legs were splayed almost 180 degrees and ended in strong, elegantly pointed bare feet. As student dancers flowed in, he got up and moved to the door, looking like a Greek God — powerful, deliberate, fluid. Feeling self-conscious, I took a spot at the back.

A woman with long, dark brown hair in a ponytail, a slim, toned body, and legs that went on forever greeted the young man by name as he left the room. I wondered if he was her boyfriend. She seemed kind of schoolmarmish as she took her place at the front of the room, her back to the mirrored wall. She removed her glasses and held them over her head up to the light. She polished the lenses with her leotard, rechecked the lenses, put the glasses back on, sat on the floor, and stretched her legs. The accompanist entered and took his seat at the piano. The studio was now full, and I was thankful I wasn't the only guy.

"Welcome. For those of you who are new, my name is Trish."

Patricia Beatty, my first modern dance instructor, was one of the founders of Toronto Dance Theatre. She took us through a series of exercises, beginning with sitting on the floor, connecting breath with movement: inhalation with expansion and a feeling of release, lightness, openness, and vulnerability; and exhalation with contraction, moving inward, getting smaller, tighter, heavier physically, and more intense emotionally. This alternation proceeded according to a count and tempo set by Trish and kept by the pianist, who improvised. At first, my body felt stiff and unresponsive. After thirty minutes on the floor, we came to standing. By then I was feeling lighter, energized. Was it my imagination or did the piano riffs now seem fuller? As instructed, I breathed in, lifted my arms above my head and opened them while looking up. Trish said to feel like we were suspended from an imaginary string from the centre of the chest.

"Give yourselves to the sky. That's it — heart high and open!"

Music filled the room and I followed, with my elbows, wrists, and fingers elongating outward. I reached toward the edges of the studio, then exhaled and folded back into myself before surfacing and extending once again. When we began shifting our weight and moving, I felt awkward, stumbled, then recovered. When we started turning, I felt my confidence surge. With arms spread wide, I whirled around on one leg as if trying to catch my other leg, which was raised slightly off the floor. The second side was more challenging but no less exhilarating. I was flushed with optimism, confident I could learn and grow there. This was a place where I could be myself, freely, joyfully, and without fear of censure. Had I found a home?

Dance became more necessary to me than ever, and I continued taking classes at TDT. Trish emphasized the importance of technique, 90 percent of which gets lost, she said, in performance. Long before the days of kinesiology studies and widespread knowledge of body mechanics, modern dance technique was approached through metaphor and image. Martha Graham, the American modern dance pioneer who invented the technique that was being taught at TDT, was a master at this and often quoted by Trish.

"All movement originates from the pelvis — from the Greek, meaning bowl, the basin from which the life force emanates."

"The spine is like the tree of life."

"Our arms, according to Martha, start from the back because they were once wings."

Yes, and I was learning to fly. I was getting more stretched out, stronger, more fluid. Classes were ninety minutes long, beginning with floor exercises, standing work, standing combinations, then combinations with dancers moving in pairs diagonally across the room, all accompanied by live piano or conga drums. The workout was gruelling but fun, would build in energy from the floor (the earth), progress upward, and climax in leaps that traversed with speed and grace the studio's floor and air space. Classes would literally soar by.

I was in class one evening when Trish singled me out. "Look at you, Sam. You're dancing! I've never seen a beginner who actually dances." I was fit to burst.

Quotes from Martha continued to regale and edify.

"The body says what words cannot."

"Movement never lies."

"It takes five years to learn to run, ten years to learn to walk, and fifteen years to stand still."

I didn't know anything about Martha at this point — whether she was living or dead, in Toronto or elsewhere — but she clearly had something going on, and I was eager to learn more. Running came naturally to me. It would take many more years than Martha predicted before I could simply stand still.

* * *

Gilda moved into Rochdale College, which had just opened as an ad hoc freewheeling university and residence with communal areas. After feeling like a misfit at Forest Hill Collegiate, she was eager to learn, and the informal promise of Rochdale classes suited her well. She always carried a small hardbound notebook with blank pages on which she sketched and recorded poems, gorgeously, with liquid ink pens. She shared a bathroom with Bernie Langer, who, despite his Jewish-sounding name, was a blond, blue-eyed, rosy-cheeked nineteen-year-old German, physically the ideal of Hitler Youth. He was vibrant and incredibly friendly, never without a book in his hands, a voracious reader who devoured Franz Kafka and Thomas Mann in the original German as easily as he savoured Kurt Vonnegut and James Joyce. In addition to Mahler and other classical music, he would play "Ducks on a Pond" by The Incredible String Band and Bob Dylan's album *Nashville Skyline*, which included Dylan singing with Johnny Cash on "Girl from the North Country." Bernie was fun to be around, had a booming laugh, loved to discuss what he was reading, smoke dope, and drop mescaline or MDA. I loved spending time with him and Gilda.

One day, I introduced my mother to Bernie when we passed by my parents' apartment to pick up mail. My nervousness was unwarranted. Bernie was courteous and friendly, as I expected he would be, and my mother was, too. Her attitude reminded me of the time I visited her in the hospital and how warm she was with the non-Jewish woman sharing her room.

The next time Luba saw me, she asked about my German friend and I told her he was doing well. He was making pottery in a rented farmhouse on Georgian Bay, in a barn where he'd set up a wheel.

"Ay, an artist. Better he should go to school."

Bernie was living the hippie dream. Every once in a while, he would come into the city and stop by, or I'd go up to Waubaushene for the weekend and a swim. Once, as we said goodbye, he kissed me just to see what that would be like. He laughed and left.

On another visit home, I told my mother that Bernie had decided to go to university and enrolled at York. She was pleased that something had knocked some sense into him. I told her he'd moved to a place in Maple, just north of the school, from where he could commute. He now had a girlfriend named Debbie, also going to York.

"Debbie? A Jewish girl?"

I honestly didn't know.

A short time later, I went to spend the day with my friends, Alvin and Glenna Rebick, who lived in a small flat above a store near the Harbord Bakery. I felt close to the couple, had danced at their wedding in a duet I choreographed to Crosby, Stills & Nash's "Wooden Ships." But when I arrived at their place that morning, they were not their usual warm and cheerful selves. Alvin especially seemed distressed to see me. He said he'd just received a call from Debbie, who was trying to find me. He said he hated to be the one giving me this news — my friend Bernie was dead, hit by a train while driving to York University.

I didn't believe it. Alvin looked down and said how sorry he was.

Tears flowed quickly through my confusion. I couldn't fathom that someone so young, so full of joie de vivre — someone I was so close to — could have been removed from the world in an instant. That I would never see him again. I staggered into the living room, flopped down on the couch, and wept. I remember looking up and thinking of Bernie as an angel, hovering and watching over us, an image absorbed from childhood church escapades. I found the thought not absurd but comforting. I was consoled by Glenna and Alvin, who were present and loving.

I hadn't seen my parents for a while. When I did, my mother, as usual, was in the kitchen.

I asked her if she remembered my friend Bernie. She didn't know who I was talking about. When I mentioned he was the "blond boy" who had visited once, she nodded. I told her that on his way to school, he was hit by a train and killed.

"He's dead, Mom."

I waited to get a reaction, as if revealing that death had touched me would come as a shock to her. Maybe she'd find a way to deny this really happened? Maybe Bernie being German would somehow nullify for her the unjustness of his sudden passing? Or was I hoping this would prompt her to reveal her own loss of loved ones, and then we could commiserate? There was a moment of silence.

"He seemed like a nice boy."

"I saw him just the other day."

"I'm sorry, Semele."

It surprised and comforted me that my mother was so sympathetic. Still, I looked to her for more.

"I don't know how to handle this."

Her lips narrowed, she shook her head and opened the refrigerator door.

I left as quickly as I could. I was completely unprepared to deal with death, had been sheltered from it. I was at a loss as to how to grieve his passing. I didn't know Bernie's family, didn't know how or if I should reach out to his parents or his sister. No one got in touch with me about a funeral. I don't know if I would have gone anyway. Anyway, Bernie was just gone. From this world. From my life.

8

Abroad

MY FATHER, ASIDE FROM HIS ROTE INSISTENCE on my becoming a doctor, never took interest in my education except once when I was in grade ten and he, inexplicably, came to the school on parents' night and spoke to my homeroom teacher. Mrs. Russell told him I had a facility for languages and should be studying German, in addition to the French and Latin I was already taking. My father had a great sense of irony; he encouraged me to go for it.

It was already late in the school year, but Mrs. Russell gave me the German textbook and left me on my own to catch up to the rest of the class, which I did, my German initially sounding more than *a bisl* like Yiddish. I studied German for another two years in high school before continuing with it in university, where I majored in modern languages and literature — Moderns, as Mrs. Russell called it, to distinguish it from Classics.

The summer following my first university year, I went on an exchange program set up by the University of Toronto's Department of German. The Lufthansa flight to Frankfurt was subsidized and a temporary job in Bavaria arranged. I packed some tabs of LSD and James Joyce's *Ulysses*, which at over seven hundred pages, weighed about a kilo and took up a good portion of my rucksack. I stayed with a family in Oberammergau and sold rolls of Agfa film and postcards to tourists in a souvenir shop outside Schloss Linderhof, not far from Neuschwanstein. These were two of Mad King Ludwig's castles, the former inspired by Versailles, the latter, inspiration for Sleeping Beauty's abode and Walt Disney's signature logo. The picturesque alpine village, with its quaint cottages adorned with flora and fauna hand painted on shutters, had me happily thinking I was sojourning in the land of fairy tales. I had no awareness that I was billeted in the town famous for its Passion Plays, in which, once every decade, the reason for hating Jews as Christ-killers was hammered home.

I was a foreigner but not unwelcome, and I felt strangely at home. Every evening, the family I was with — mom, dad, and daughter Karola — gathered around the TV for a *Krimi*, a crime thriller that had them hooked. Other times we played word games. It amazed them that I not only remembered but could pronounce ridiculous compound words like *Berufsmässigertrauernder*, which meant a professional mourner. They kept asking me to say the word and laughed every time I managed to spit it out.

On a day off from work, I found my way into a meadow in the foothills of the Bavarian Alps and, with no trees nearby, plopped myself down on a patch of grass in full sun. I dropped a hit of acid and started to read *Ulysses*. It seemed only moments before I went volcanic, erupted in a laughing fit, too stoned to follow what I was reading but not too stoned to trip out on the words. I didn't care if any moocows were watching. Like the well-trained student I was, I had started at the beginning, intending to read the pages in order, but now the front of the book or the back was a matter of indifference to me. I got stuck on Molly Bloom's soliloquy. "Yes! Yes! Yes!" I shouted out to the hills. I waited for the echo to return, but none came until what seemed like minutes later. I saw myself from above, an aerial shot of a solitary figure, legs crossed in an open field in Bavaria, reading and laughing and alone. I was doing a Bernie.

After three weeks of mornings resisting invitations to slather more butter on the deliciously dense German rye bread, I made my *auf Wiedersehens* and set off. I hitchhiked to Venice where I checked into a youth hostel. I spent the day on the sandy beach of the Lido and garnered a painful sunburn. I had to delay leaving Venice for my hitchhiking tour across western Europe, my back and shoulders too burnt to bear a backpack.

A multicultural array of people stayed at the hostel. Among them, the requisite Australian taking two years off to do a world tour. Another was a long-haired young German man who had a guitar on his back. I overheard someone ask him in German why he answered in English.

"I will never speak German."

"Doch bist du Deutsch, nicht wahr?" (But you are German, no?)

"I am a student of history. Knowing my country's history, I refuse to have anything to do with it. Even speaking its language I find repugnant."

I also met a sweet Swedish girl named Neta who was a rare Swede with dark hair and dark eyes, which was one of the reasons she was happy to be abroad. Neta told me she was about to head out across northern Italy and along the French Riviera. We decided to make the journey together.

After hitchhiking along the Mediterranean coast, we reached Algeciras and hopped on an overnight ferry to Morocco. We headed to Marrakesh, in those days replete with zoned-out hippies in full-length jellabas, heads shrouded under hoods, eyes shielded behind sunglasses. They sat in favourite cafés around the main square, the Jemaa el-Fnaa, high on kif and God knows what else, drinking tea out of glasses stuffed with fresh mint leaves, or nursing in slow motion glasses of sweet milky coffee laced with black pepper. People were generous, even with their kif. We stuffed some of the loose leaves we'd been given into a pipe bowl and lit up, too. The dope was potent, and we quickly got stoned.

There were drummers and magicians, cobras and snake charmers in the square and, in the labyrinthine souk, hawkers eager to bargain their wares. Later we would each buy for a few dirham collarless slip-on shirts of white muslin with white embroidery on the placket and, for our bell-bottom jeans, dark brown leather belts studded with rows of silver grommets. The most mundane of objects looked exotic, like the bottles of Coca-Cola riddled with Arabic lettering offsetting the familiar logo script. Some people spoke French, most Arabic. We were definitely on another continent.

We found a cheap hotel with a tiny room and a bed full of bedbugs that feasted on us when we lay down in the afternoon heat. It was too hot to move, too hot even to swat away the bugs. Still, we managed to fall asleep.

In the cooler evening, we got up, wandered about, scratching our bites, loving the soft wind. It felt like a small desert town, surrounded as it was by a wall of pinky-red clay, the Atlas Mountains not twenty miles away, limning the southern sky with dark shadows.

We decided to spend a day chilling outside the city. We sauntered just beyond the walls on the main road. In the distance, sleek Arabians thundered, kicking up sand like a scene out of *Lawrence of Arabia*. We stopped to admire the horsemanship. Rifles were fired into the sky from barrelling riders dressed in white, red fabric belts, and tassels horizontal in the wind.

Waves of people, many with their families, strolled outside the old town enjoying the day. It felt benign, safe. I asked Neta if she wanted to try some acid. She said yes. We each dropped a hit, thinking the LSD would intensify the weirdness of the scene even more. Which it did.

Neta started feeling a little queasy, dizzy. We found a space in the shade by the side of the main road, near an area with some shrubbery, where we sat down on the trunk of a felled palm. Soon a Moroccan man appeared and sat nearby. He asked me questions in French about where we were from, how we liked Morocco, and other such things. I answered candidly, marvelling at how friendly the people were. He asked me about Neta. I told him she was not Canadian, but from Sweden.

"Mais vous êtes mariés, non? Elle est votre femme."

"Non. Elle n'est pas ma femme. Elle est mon amie."

"Ah, oui?"

"Oui."

I was getting a kick out of being able to communicate in French, even if it was rudimentary.

"Votre amie, elle ne vas pas bien?"

"Pardon?"

"Elle est malade?"

"Non, elle n'est pas malade. Un peu trop de soleil, c'est tout."

"Alors, elle est propre?"

"Propre?"

"Oui, pas sale."

I was tripping out. Why was he asking me if Neta was dirty? Her grooming habits were excellent. Instead of taking offence, I tried to edify him.

"Non, bien sûr, elle n'est pas sale."

Just then several men emerged from the bushes. We were too stoned to react in a big way but fear rose in my gut. I was afraid I had said too much.

"Neta, let's get out of here."

I took her arm to leave, but we were surrounded by eight men. A couple of them grabbed my arms and held them behind my back. Others pulled Neta aside, separating us.

The situation was unreal, surreal. I felt like I was being held under water, every movement requiring supreme effort. I managed to free myself and yell, "Neta, run. Run!" I was hoping my shouting would scare them off or alert some passerby to our distress. But I looked up and noticed it was almost dark and the area, but for these men, was deserted. Neta was on the ground, over near the bushes. I fought to get to her, pushing away the guys near me.

"Neta! Neta!"

"Don't fight, Sam. Don't fight. It's okay."

Still, I struggled. Time seemed to have slowed down. I looked at one of the men next to me. He looked young, with the scruffy beard of a teenager. He had his penis in his hand and was jerking off on me.

"What the fuck?"

It was then I realized what a fool I'd been.

"J'ai menti! Elle est sale! Elle est sale, malade. J'ai menti!" (I lied! She is unclean! She is unclean, sick. I lied!)

The men started to disperse into the brush. I grabbed Neta's hand, pulled her up. We ran out into the middle of the road and headed toward the town's gate. As we ran, I turned, looked back, saw nothing. The road was dark, no one about. I plumbed my memory for how to say "Help!" in French. There was a story we'd read in grade eight about a plane that crashed in the Pyrenees near Perpignan. I remembered and mimicked what the survivors had shouted, *"Aux secours! Aux secours!"*

My voice was swallowed by the night. Finally, in the distance, headlights appeared. I waved my arms frantically, but the car didn't stop. Another car sped by. Then another. We must have been a sight. Neta said she was not hurt but looked disheveled. I was convinced I was covered in blood, clothes torn and filthy. Another headlight. I started yelling again. This time the car stopped. It was a taxi. I opened the door and we jumped in. I explained in breathless French that we were attacked by a group of men. I implored the driver to please hurry and get us out of there and back to our hotel. I didn't know if we were being pursued. The driver said, *"Bien sûr,"* but first he wanted to know what they did to us. Something in the way he asked weirded me out. And the leer in his eyes.

"Neta, we have to get out of here. Quick! Let's go!"

Before a word could pass her lips, we jumped out of the taxi and continued to run like hell. I was convinced the driver would have taken us somewhere and the assault repeated. Oh my God, I thought. We were all alone. There was no help for us anywhere. I was afraid to ask Neta what they did to her. I said we'd try and find a doctor as soon as we got back to the hotel.

Neta said not to worry, she was all right. Still, we ran. I don't know how we managed to make it to the hotel, but we did. Exhausted, we went up to our room. Neta went to the toilet first. I looked at myself in the mirror and was horrified. Not a cut or scratch anywhere. I looked around for a weapon, a knife, anything with a sharp edge, desperate to draw blood. I started pummelling myself, tearing at my skin with my fingernails, scratching my face, my arms. I was bleeding now and I cried. I cried because I had not been hurt. I cried because I'd failed to protect Neta.

The next day, after entering and quickly exiting a filthy local hospital, we found a private doctor that our hotel concierge recommended. He was from France but spoke English as well. We sat in his office and told him what had happened but left out the part about the drugs. He yelled at us, particularly at me.

"How could you be so stupid? Don't you know this is a Third World country?"

"Of course, but —"

"It's dangerous outside the city walls! No one ventures there once the sun goes down! I've never encountered such idiocy."

I asked the doctor to please examine Neta to make sure she was all right.

"The people here are sexually repressed and deprived. They will do anything when given a chance.... Come with me."

Neta followed the doctor into an examination room. I waited in agony. How could I have been so reckless? After what seemed like an hour, they returned. Neta smiled at me meekly, then looked down at the floor.

"As far as I can tell, except for some abrasions, I think she is okay. There may be long-term problems, I don't know. I advise she see her family doctor as soon as she gets back home to make sure there aren't any hidden issues. I recommend taking it easy for a few days. You are both very foolish and very lucky. You could just as easily have been killed."

I asked how much we owed him.

"Nothing, just promise me you will use some common sense and take care."

I didn't know what to say to Neta about what had happened, so I said nothing. She didn't speak about it either. We left Morocco and headed back across Spain, this time up to Madrid. I never thought I'd be happy to get back to Spain, with Franco's jackbooted soldiers posted at crossroads, wearing full military regalia, hard shiny flat-topped hats with chinstraps, machine guns slung over their shoulders. Okay, maybe not happy, but relieved. Madrid seemed different from what we'd seen of Spain, seemed like an international city, somehow less repressed. I loved the parks and statues, the wide, elegant boulevards. We went to the Prado Museum and spent time in front of the Goyas. *Saturn Devouring His Son* struck a chord with me.

In Paris, we stayed in a tiny hotel with cardboard walls and more bedbugs. I was not as taken by the city as I thought I'd be. I think it was my state of mind. Still, I sat in a bistro and ordered a Ricard, then a café au lait. Felt the echo of Baudelaire, Rimbaud, Apollinaire. I made my way to 52 rue du Louvre, the central post office and the counter with the "Post Restante" sign. There I received mail from home with my marks for first year university. I laughed at the ridiculousness of having been assessed grades in French and German, particularly absurd considering where I was, what I'd gone through. If not completely fluent, hadn't I been getting by? What did a B mean in Linguistics? Or an A minus in German literature?

It was July 1969, and we were in Paris when the first men landed on the moon. And it was in Paris where Neta and I took large steps and parted ways — Neta back to Sweden, I to London, from where my return flight to Toronto was to depart. It was an awkward goodbye, ridden with guilt and regret and the callowness of a youth not yet nineteen years old. We promised to stay in touch.

* * *

When I returned from Europe, I consulted my brother the doctor about a genital problem. He suggested the venereal diseases clinic at Toronto General. I went and a swab was taken, tests were done. I was given a prescription to fill. On my way out, I happened to see Chris, the English guy who had turned me on to *Sgt. Pepper's*. He beamed at me like a fellow traveller.

"You too, eh?"

I smiled and offered a shit-happens shrug. I didn't tell him it was a run-of-the mill urinary tract infection and not a dose of the clap.

I went home for a visit. Removing my shoes at the door, as was our custom, I entered the living room. Nothing had changed except for the addition of a transparent plastic sheet covering the light gold broadloom. Fitted plastic slipcovers still protected the white lampshades and the faux French provincial furniture. In the adjoining dining room sat my father, my mother behind him, standing as always. They had company from the old country, a landsman I hadn't met. He was reserved and soft-spoken. My father asked me, "Did you *sprechen Sie Deutsch*?"

"*Jawohl, mein Herr!*"

He snorted out a laugh. All through school, I had this game that never failed to send him into paroxysms of laughter. I'd say something innocuous and sweet in German like "Mother, can I please have a glass of water," but I would do it in the German of a Nazi barking orders: "*Mutti, bitte geben Sie mir ein Glas Wasser!*" My father would double over in hysterics, not able to talk for minutes until, finally catching his breath, he'd wipe the tears from his eyes and settle down. Then he'd have me do it again.

I told my parents that the people I worked for in Germany were very nice and they sent along their heartfelt best wishes. My parents nodded, and the landsman shifted in his chair and muttered, "I hear the trains in Germany are also very nice."

"Oh, I couldn't afford to take a train. I had to hitchhike to get around. I even had to skip meals to save money."

Red-faced, the landsman lifted his gaze to the ceiling, trying to maintain his composure.

I carried on regardless, saying I once went a whole day without eating, then mumbled something about now understanding what suffering meant.

"Suffering?" the man shouted. "You call that suffering?"

The loudness and suddenness of his eruption stunned me into silence.

"What do you know about suffering? What do you know? Huh? Tell me!"

"Sorry. I was just ..."

I caught sight of a tattoo peeking out from under his rolled shirtsleeves. It was a number and it was screaming at me. And

I was ashamed. That, unlike my parents, he said something —
alluded to his own traumatic history — jolted me. The man's
reaction came from a zone where hunger was not a noun but
a verb, growling with hollow, angry letters. My travels had
taken me to dark places, but I couldn't shake the feeling that
they were light years from where he — and my parents — had
been. I had travelled to West Berlin and seen the ruins of the
Reichstag and the shells of countless other bombed-out build-
ings like the tower of the Kaiser Wilhelm Memorial Church
on the Kudamm in the heart of the city. They were haunting
but mute, and did not reveal to me their innermost tales. I had
crossed Checkpoint Charlie into East Berlin and seen people
gathered on a bridge looking over into the water as if someone
had just jumped in. *"Was ist geschehen?"* I asked several on-
lookers but no one would answer, not the babushka'd woman
carrying a basket of potatoes from the market, not the man in
the ragg wool driving cap. Were these dark and silent places
close to the land my parents and their friend once inhabited?
And what happened to them there? I wanted to know but did
not ask. Because there was one thing I did know — I knew
there would be no answer.

9

Waving Free

I DECIDED TO QUIT SEEING THE SHRINK WITH the pipe. I survived my trip abroad, I could survive without a safety net or having to pay for fifty minutes of studied silence coming from behind a desk. I rented a room with a shared kitchen and bathroom on the second floor of a house on Brunswick Avenue. I was out in the world on my own, ready to dive into my life with relish, eager to follow my passion.

Continuing in second year of Moderns at the University of Toronto, I found my courses, like Chaucer, irrelevant, meaningless, absurd. Liberation and relevance were the mantras of the day. What was the point of studying classical French tragic theatre? How would Racine and Corneille help me to live a life that was true to myself?

I felt a pull away from academics into something more vital and alive. I started skipping classes, ignoring assignments, and saw my putative professorship fading from the future. But I didn't tell my parents.

I began taking dance classes every day at the Toronto Dance Theatre. There were a number of us that were serious about dance and showing some promise. We coalesced into a group of scholarship students with free tuition: Larry McKinnon, Kathryn Brown, Mary Newberry, Colleen May, Kathy Phillips, David Wood. We were taught by Trish and the other founders of TDT, Peter Randazzo, who had been in the Martha Graham Company in the sixties, and David Earle, the erudite choreographer with a liturgical bent. We also took classes from TDT company members: Susan Macpherson, Keith Urban, Amelia Itcush, Barry Smith, soon to be joined by Helen Jones, Kathy Wildberger, and Merle Salsberg. Donald Himes (composer of CBC's *Mr. Dressup* theme song) taught us Dalcroze Eurythmics.

Our cohort developed a kind of closeness based on shared experiences and interests. Kathryn was a budding astrologer who taught me the computations to make birth charts. I soaked it up, not just the math but the symbolism. I was intrigued by how closely each of us displayed the characteristics of our respective signs. Kathryn, a Leo, was radiant like the sun, imperial like a lion with the hauteur of a Nubian goddess, a buoyant dancer who commanded attention with an insouciant flick of the wrist. Kathryn discovered I was a vegetarian like her. She invited me for dinner to her mother's house in an upscale area of Leaside. Her mother was passionate about the arts and recently divorced from Kathryn's father, whose signature, as Secretary of the Treasury of Jamaica, was on its paper money. She cooked us a typical Jamaican meal but without the meat: curried vegetables and rice and peas (red kidney beans). I loved the flavour but couldn't get past the spicy heat of the food, not being used to it. So not Jewish! Kathryn tossed back her head and laughed. "It's really a very mild curry," she said in her mid-Atlantic accent.

Also a Leo, David Wood had narrow shoulders and well-developed haunches and a flame-coloured mane of hair arcing above his freckled face. He'd had some ballet training and moved like a satyr. He didn't suffer fools gladly, was cynical and arch. Larry, by contrast, was shy but friendly and eager. He'd moved from Alberta to study dance at the TDT. He was a Libra, like me, and serious about art. Kathy Phillips was an Aries, the polar opposite of Libra. She was elfin, direct, and to the point but with a mischievous sense of humour and a wicked laugh. She was living with Robert Flanagan, an up-and-coming Toronto poet published by the House of Anansi. Colleen, by contrast, was tall and thin, with a long neck like many Tauruses, including Trish Beatty. She was elegant in her movement and showed much promise as a choreographer. Mary had a background in Highland dancing. She looked mousy, as many Virgos do, but once on stage, transformed into a virago that you couldn't not look at. Mary's parents were Quakers. Her mother was Jo Vellacott, an academic interested in women's rights; her father, a doctor committed to treating First Nations people poisoned by the mercury pollution on the Grassy Narrows reserve. My parents, I didn't want to talk about.

Around Easter, we put on a satirical show at the St. Lawrence Centre, called *Ham'n Eggs*. It was silly and fun, mostly romping around the stage, close to naked. To justify my dance studies, I happened to mention to my mother something about the performance, but I told her it was just a workshop and to please not come, not that my parents would. This time, of course, they showed up. Were they expecting my boyhood Charlie Chaplin routine? Well, they got to see me dance nude except for a dance belt (jock strap) with my bare ass hanging out. I was mortified.

My father wasn't exactly thrilled either. He tried to bribe me to move back home. Said he would buy me a car. I laughed at the suggestion. What did I need a car for when I lived downtown and could walk or take public transit everywhere?

He didn't yet know I wanted to become a professional dancer, and when he found out I was dropping out of university, he was livid. He said he'd rent me an apartment. All I had to do was go back to school. This bribe also held no water for me.

One day, I got a letter from Neta. She still didn't feel at home in Sweden and now wanted to emigrate to Canada. I encouraged her to do so, telling her she could stay with me. I felt conflicted, simultaneously hoping she would come and that she wouldn't be able to make it. I still felt guilty about the sexual assault in Morocco; there was unfinished business between us. Neta arrived in Toronto and moved in with me. Although only a single room, it was large with a double mattress on the floor and a small table I used as a desk.

Suddenly it felt like I was married. I would go to classes, either at the university or at TDT, for most of the day, then return home. Neta would have dinner waiting for me. She was still reserved but determined to forge a new life. She practised her English, made friends with my friends. Evenings, we would chat, read, have sex. She didn't seem at all inhibited or twisted by her experiences. Finally, I screwed up the courage to ask her.

"What did your family doctor in Sweden say?"

"Not too much."

"Well, he examined you, didn't he?"

"Yes."

"What did he tell you?"

"It's not important."

"Neta, I need to know."

"He told me that I won't be able to bear children."

Not the words I'd been hoping to hear.

"I am so sorry. I don't know what to say. I'm so sorry."

Neta shrugged it off. She told me that having children was not a high priority for her.

"Anyway, I don't know if he is correct."

I took Neta to meet my favourite aunt, who had spent some of the war and later years in Sweden. Auntie Sallah was delighted.

"*Välkommen, Neta!*" (Welcome, Neta!)

"Thank you, Mrs. Chaiton."

"Please call me Sallah. *Du kan prata svenska med mig.*" (You can speak Swedish with me.)

"*Tack. Tack så mycket.*" (Thank you.)

Neta tried teaching me some Swedish, but I couldn't master the breathing. Somehow she was able to speak on inhalation, as if Swedish words were created by sucking air in rather than expelling it. Sallah obviously had no problem with that as she talked about her sister, who was still living in Stockholm.

I was happy that Neta could speak her mother tongue to someone — not just someone but my favourite aunt. And I was delighted that my aunt seemed rejuvenated when recalling the language of her liberation.

My father's reaction was another matter. One day, he dropped by our place unannounced. He came up the stairs to our room. I introduced him to Neta, who asked if he'd like some tea and then quickly disappeared down the hall into the kitchen. My father surveyed the place with a grimace of disgust. He looked down at my mattress and kicked it, muttering a curse in Yiddish ("*farfluchte* …"), and shooting me the dirtiest look. Funny, I was thinking he might be begrudgingly proud of me, being so young and worldly, living with a beautiful woman. But he wasn't.

"*Got shtruft!*" (God punishes!) he hissed at me.

I had transgressed, what I don't know. Maybe that Neta was a shiksa and Jewish boys joked and dreamed of what shiksas were supposedly good for. But I don't think it was prurience on my father's part. Was it because I was no longer going to school? Maybe it was my undeniable bohemianism that irked him. Was he pissed that I would settle for a mattress on a floor in a rooming house when he was offering me a life of relative luxury with my own apartment? Or was he thinking of his own lost youth, or the youth he never had? Was he jealous?

Neta and I split up soon thereafter. We both felt trapped in a relationship that had no future. But not because I wanted to have children, which I didn't. No future because I felt so guilty given what had happened in the past and given my father's venomous words, against which I had no antidote. Neta moved in with my friends Alvin and Glenna.

I lost track of Neta, not consciously or on purpose, but probably deliberately. She hooked up with Mark Lam, my first roommate and a Libra who looked somewhat like me, and they ended up getting married. They also had a baby. Hearing this news, how glad I felt for Neta, how relieved for myself.

* * *

My brother David called me one evening, freaking out. He was having a bad acid trip, hallucinating and scared. I told him to hang in there, it would pass.

"I'll be there as fast as the TTC will take me."

I asked David if he could walk the five blocks to Mister Donut at the corner of Bathurst and Wilson, where we could meet. He said, "Okay but hurry." I didn't want our parents to freak about the drugs or to hope my sudden appearance in their neck of the woods meant I was returning to the fold.

David was sitting at a small table in the doughnut shop when I arrived. He tried, with only partial success, to stand up, gave me a big off-kilter smile and we hugged. His blazing eyes looked manic, but he felt more like himself, if very stoned.

"Far out afro, Samarama." Since moving out, I had grown out my hair into an electric Jimi Hendrix afro.

David didn't want to talk about anything personal or heavy. He just wanted me to be there for him as he came down.

I removed the army surplus greatcoat I was wearing and pulled out a book from my knapsack. It was *The House at Pooh Corner* by A.A. Milne, a book I loved as a child and a classic I'd been rereading, its Zen wisdom even more resonant now, particularly when high. I wasn't high, but David was up for me taking him on a trip with Winnie the Pooh and his friends.

I got us some coffee and treats. I read aloud to David while he dipped a cruller into his coffee and I nibbled on a chocolate coconut doughnut. From the very start, when Pooh went to search for Piglet at his house, found the door open and yet no Piglet, we laughed at the naive but profound wisdom of the characters.

"The more he looked, the more Piglet wasn't there."

"Oh yeah. I can dig this!" said David, slouching back in the chair.

David's restless mind found a perfect place to settle, with good-natured humour and universal truths aplenty. For a couple of hours, we revelled in the *is*-ness of Pooh's being and of life in general, as David gradually relaxed. It was an extraordinary trip, brimming with laughter and brotherhood, both of us relishing the innocence of childhood and a sense that all was right with the world if we could just — whatever. I was gratified that I was able to offer him some of the guidance, protection, love, and care we both needed. David's warmth toward me made me blush. We parted ways — he to our parents' place, me back downtown — feeling as tight as conspirators after a successful heist.

* * *

I decided to dance full-time and drop out of university, only three second-year credits completed. Then I found out my name had been omitted from the new list of scholarship students at the TDT school. I was crushed, couldn't believe it. I had all my eggs in this basket! I screwed up my courage to speak to David and Peter. In tears, I told them how important dancing was to me; that it had become my life, that I'd quit university and needed the free tuition as a scholarship student. They seemed surprised and had no inkling how committed I was. I'd never articulated it. I had thought my actions spoke volumes of my intention: regularly taking two classes a day, indeed never missing any, showing up for rehearsals early, with focus and enthusiasm.

But upon reflection, I realize that declaring my desire openly and clearly had always been difficult for me given my background, where my wants could not honestly be expressed without consequence. In the face of what my parents had suffered (as unspecific and hidden as it was), how did I dare allow myself to want anything that would hurt them? So I cultivated a deliberate vagueness about what I really wanted. But that day, because I had nothing left to lose, I managed to declare myself to David and Peter, and my scholarship was renewed.

Guiding my actions, but also undeclared, was my longing for a family dictated not by blood ties but by free association, with relationships built on mutual respect, love, and trust. Only dimly aware that was what I was searching for, I came to live in a commune on Beverly Street just north of Queen Street with Alvin, Glenna, and a few other friends. We pooled resources for food and shared chores like shopping and cleaning. I felt loved and accepted for who I was, and I continued with my dance training. Fellow dance student Mary Newberry lived in another commune around the corner on Soho Street. My parents never came to visit; neither did my brothers, who thought I'd gone total hippie.

I was invited to Abie and Sue's house for dinner, to celebrate my belated birthday. When I got there, only Sue was at home. She was finishing the dinner preparations and told me that Abie was running late at work but should be home soon. He was a resident, working in Emergency at a downtown hospital. Sue and I chatted for a while and, as the clock ticked on, she became more and more agitated by his absence. I didn't mind. I'd set aside the entire evening and I liked Sue and her gregariousness. Once, when I was younger, we'd gone out for an evening of drinks and jazz at Stop 33, at the top of the Sutton Place Hotel, and I felt very grown up. Now I was asking her about her sociology studies (she already had a nursing degree), especially Deviance and Social Control, the course that I was most interested in, having audited a couple of classes with her dynamic professor, Ian Currie, whose lectures were extraordinarily engaging.

Hours passed and the dinner got cold. Abie finally walked in the door, haggard. Head down, he shuffled to the closet and removed his jacket while monotoning quiet, measured responses to Sue's rapid fire, in an exchange I found unforgettable.

"You're two hours late!"

"I couldn't leave."

"Of course you could leave. Your shift was over hours ago."

"I couldn't leave. There was a teenage kid —"

"I don't care who was there. Someone else could have taken over."

"There was nobody else."

"One of the largest hospitals in the city and there's nobody else?"

"He had overdosed."

"So? This happens all the time."

"He was dying."

"Sam is here. He's been waiting patiently for you. For ages. You invited him over for a birthday dinner that's now ruined."

"The kid was dying. I couldn't just leave him."

Abie was crushed and I wanted to die.

"Did he die?"

"Yes."

"Well, did you wash your hands afterward? Did you wash your hands? Go scrub your hands before you come in here!"

I thanked my lucky Libran stars that I never became a doctor or a husband, made my excuses, and fled.

10

Beneath the Diamond Sky

I FLEW TO NEW YORK TO TAKE CLASSES AT THE Graham studio on East Sixty-Third Street. I threw caution to the wind and signed up for a master class with Martha herself. She entered, hobbling on a cane, ancient, and in full makeup, her hair pulled tight to the back of her head in a wide chignon. She sat, back upright, on a low bench in front of the mirrored wall in the large studio. Her introduction was brief, barely a welcome before she launched into the ritual of her technique.

"Bounces, breathings on two and four, openings on three …"

Martha's presence was intimidating, formidable, and I was more than a little afraid. I cursed myself for thinking I was up for this, but proud, too, that I had the chutzpah to even try it. That is, until after the floor work when doing our standing exercises; the slight raise of her bony hand brought the movement and piano accompaniment to an abrupt halt.

"You."

I turned around and looked behind me to the back of the class and realized that all sixty eyes of the dancers in the studio were staring at me. I wanted to crawl into a corner and disappear.

"Where are you from?"

"Canada. Toronto."

"Toronto? Peter Randazzo is your teacher?"

"Yes, ma'am."

"Well, he should know better."

The movement we were doing begins *en attitude* with a pelvic contraction that pulls the raised bent leg forward and in toward the navel, and the release sends it back and up in a repeating figure eight pattern that is mirrored by the movement of the opposite arm. But not according to Martha.

"Clytemnestra is deciding whether to go ahead and kill Agamemnon, her husband who had sacrificed their daughter to appease the Goddess of the Hunt, before sailing for Troy. Clytemnestra is weighing both sides of the argument, the agony of a yes-or-no decision, forgiveness or retribution, life or death. That is what is at stake here, and you are not showing me that. Now, once more. With focus."

* * *

When I returned to Toronto, I took more agency in my development as a dance artist. Pierre Trudeau's Liberal government had just initiated a program to combat youth unemployment called Opportunities for Youth, as well as a related job creation stimulus called the Local Initiatives Program. I applied for and received a grant to form a dance collective, which we called The Community Dance Group, comprised of fellow scholarship students from the Toronto Dance Theatre school. We printed up flyers and lined up lecture demonstrations in local schools, enjoying a stipend, some independence, and connection to the downtown Toronto community.

Meanwhile, at the TDT school, in addition to our own classes, we served as demonstrators in lower level classes taught by TDT company members. I was busy but something was missing.

My consciousness of how I was using my body had been undergoing a radical shift during this period. After a back injury sustained in performance of a Donald Himes's piece at Ottawa's National Arts Centre, I started taking yoga classes. I went to the Sivananda Centre in Val Morin, Quebec, and then on a retreat to the Sierra Nevada mountains in northern California with Swami Vishnudevananda. I was loving it, the focus on prana, moving the body with the breath, concentration, meditation, the vegetarianism — it all fit like a glove. I was finding myself more relaxed and centred.

I went to see David Drum, a Toronto chiropractic doctor who specialized in treating dancers, to follow up on my back injury. After a brief examination, he advised me that whatever I was doing, to please continue. I took a tai chi workshop with Chungliang "Al" Huang (author of *Embrace Tiger, Return to Mountain*), who was then teaching modern dance in the fledgling dance program at York University, and I was excited about applying yogic type breathing and prana not just to static asanas but to movement. After seeing me perform, Huang told me that he loved my dancing, although he could sense some tightness in my chest and shoulders. I looked to loosen up more. Sessions in the Alexander Technique with Nehemia Cohen taught me to inhibit my usual response of retracting my head on the spine before moving and retrained me to free the tension in my neck and to move more from the joints than the muscles. The Graham technique was seeming dated, old school, cultivating tension within the body to express what was appearing to me to be not drama but melodrama.

It was then that I came across an issue of *Dance Magazine* with an article about the Hawkins technique by Beverly Brown, a lead dancer with New York City's Erick Hawkins Dance Company. It blew me away, hitting all the right notes: using the body in a more "natural" way; "not doing" instead of doing; focusing on alignment of joints and the strengthening of the psoas muscles, which connect the legs to the spine; using the arms and legs like tassels that trail responsively from the core rather than being placed or positioned as in ballet and classical modern dance; and all swathed in Eastern philosophy, Zen, and Krishnamurti. Hawkins developed this technique as a result of injuries from dancing with Graham. He had been married to Martha, was her lead male dancer and collaborator on her celebrated modern masterpieces like *Appalachian Spring*, *Cave of the Heart*, and *Night Journey*, the latter two based on Greek mythology. Hawkins had graduated from Harvard with a degree in Classics before becoming a dancer for George Balanchine's American Ballet and Ballet Caravan. I found out later that Agamemnon in Graham's *Clytemnestra* was said to represent her rancour against Hawkins, the two having recently divorced.

When I next visited New York, I decided to check out the Hawkins studio, on lower Fifth Avenue south of Fourteenth

Street. It was a small space but airy, with suspended Japanese rice paper screens floating off the wood floor to create the dressing rooms, and a single studio with windows at one end that let in natural light. I was welcomed and allowed to observe a company class taught by Erick. The dancers were warming up. One male dancer stood on one leg and extended his free leg back as if it were a tail, his arms reaching out, then folding into the body like wings, softly at the elbows and wrists. It seemed as if his joints had breath in them, and he moved with the lightness and presence of a bird. I was mesmerized and enchanted.

The class proceeded like a Graham technique class but without the muscular tension: floor work, standing work, then combinations across the floor. The vocabulary had significant differences, too. Hawkins spoke of contraction and decontraction — not contraction and release — which to my eyes had to do with a natural tensing and then relaxing of joints and musculature. At one point, the class started moving sideways across the floor in a simple chainlike pattern I had learned in Graham, with the right leg bent and reaching to the side, the left crossing over to the front, the right reaching out again, the left now crossing over to the back, all while the upper body stayed on one level facing the front. The Hawkins version was similar but notably distinct: The engine was in the lower torso, not the legs, and the arms were easy and floating, not held and placed. The torso bobbed subtly up and down in an overcurve and undercurve, a wavelike undulation that made the dancers' legs appear weightless; the pelvic muscles, like those in the haunches of the most graceful of animals, propelled the movement with quiet power. The dancers glided across the studio like a travelling whisper. Gorgeous.

* * *

I flew back to Toronto on Christmas Eve, feeling alone and lonesome, when I received a phone call from Mary Newberry asking me to Christmas dinner at her new communal house midtown near Yonge and Eglinton. I was thankful for the invitation and gladly accepted. I asked if I could bring anything, and Mary said, "Just yourself."

It being Christmas, I decided a bottle of wine and a pewter vase I had recently purchased at the Royal Ontario Museum gift shop would be perfect for the home of this group of people I had first met at Soho Street. Among them was Lisa Hetherington and Terry Swinton, who had once come to see Mary and me dance at Toronto Workshop Productions Theatre (now Buddies in Bad Times) on Alexander Street. Also living in the house was Lisa's ten-year-old son, Marty. They loved the vase and flipped over the coincidence that it was from Malaysia, where some of the group had lived and others (Terry's sister, Kathy; Eitel and Gus) still maintained a home while carrying on the group's business of importing batik fabric and upscale batik fashion clothing they designed and tailored there. The bottle of wine I brought was not so popular, although I didn't know it then, as it was graciously accepted then stashed in the kitchen, never to reappear.

The house was warm, homey, and decidedly more put together than the hippie houses downtown, with hand-knotted Moroccan rugs on the hardwood floors, lamps with shades (not plastic), and a comfortable olive velour sofa and chairs. Their boutique, called Five Believers Batiks, was in Yorkville at a time when the area was just becoming gentrified and chic. Lisa and Terry, who were ardent Bob Dylan aficionados, had taken the name from an obscure Dylan song, "Obviously Five Believers." There were five of them, good friends without any business or entrepreneurial background, who had stumbled into the business by serendipity during a trip to the Far East.

The evening sped by quickly with great food, lots of talking and laughter, no drinking and no drugs, although there was turkey and I was vegetarian. Everyone was open about themselves and their class-diverse backgrounds, which they acknowledged and joked about. Families and cultural differences were seen as tribal engines that keep people divided. Terry said that all of us were raised by our parents to feel special and more important than anyone else in the world just because we were born into their family; we just absorb that self-importance, don't even notice it, let alone question it. "Some dangerous shit, man. It's a miracle we can come together at all."

I didn't feel special or at least wouldn't admit feeling special in any way. I had a general awareness of feeling separate and apart and had questioned why. But this feeling also extended to within my family. I was aware that whenever I got stoned, I'd find myself opening up to strangers as friends, the concept of stranger suddenly incomprehensible, meaningless. What keeps us from getting close to one another? Could it be tribalism as reinforced by family, as Terry was saying, that prevents us from recognizing our common humanity?

Terry looked like the young Ron Howard, a sandy-haired and blue-eyed all-American boy, born to privilege, his mother Canadian and his father an Austrian who had represented Austria as a fencer in the Olympics. Terry attended Upper Canada College, where his classmates were people like Michael Ignatieff who was descended from Russian aristocracy and, as a Harvard professor, was to provide intellectual justification for the

U.S. invasion of Iraq and later to become, at least for a short time, the leader of the federal Liberal Party of Canada. Terry rebelled against the militarism and hierarchy promoted at the school and hated its exclusivity; nevertheless, he came to the sobering but welcomed realization that a sense of entitlement had invaded his pores, and freeing himself from that was his highest priority. His sister Kathy, raised entitled by the same parents, but as a female, felt a little less special than Terry. They had lived with their parents in lavish apartments in Knightsbridge, London, and on Park Avenue in New York City, where their father was, among other things, the president of Encyclopedia Britannica.

There also was wealth and privilege in Lisa's family, but it was the abject poverty of her childhood that marked her life. Lisa's mother, from an upper class Scottish Canadian family, died while giving birth to her; Lisa was raised in northern Ontario by a dirt-poor German father who was a fundamentalist Christian minister and ex-boxer. Lisa recalled being bullied when she was a kid not only because she was small, but because she was German, this being just after the Second World War. Her grandparents, once every year on her birthday, which was their daughter's death day, would come gliding up in their town car to the shack Lisa lived in with her father and present her with some absurdly lavish gift like a jewel-encrusted watch.

"My grandmother, who would entertain the Duke and Duchess of Windsor when they were in Toronto, would lecture me to remember who I was and warn me that people would seek me out and try to use me because of my lineage. Which was hilarious cause I was starving and didn't have shoes that fit. I sucked on coal for nourishment, for chrissake."

They asked me about my parents and my brothers, and we talked about being Jewish. Although not Jewish, Lisa seemed to be familiar with everything about the Chosen People. She even knew how to keep a kosher home, which she had learned while working as housekeeper and nanny for the Perles, an orthodox Toronto family, while she was pregnant with Marty.

I told them I had just applied for a Canada Council grant to study in Tel Aviv with the Batsheva Dance Company, a troupe that had its beginnings in the friendship between Martha Graham and Baroness Batsheva de Rothschild. My friends questioned how I would feel being in Israel, and I confessed that I never really had a desire to go there, had misgivings about it and the situation with the Palestinians, their displacement and oppression. I was not even sure I wanted to continue with the Graham technique, which is what they were then practicing at Batsheva.

Everyone in the house seemed to be genuinely interested in my life and what I was doing. I was chuffed, taken aback, overcome by the warmth and good feelings directed at me. At one point, I commented about how at home I felt, and Lisa said, "Well, you know you're going to be coming here to live with us."

I laughed nervously and shrugged it off.

*   *   *

David Earle decided to teach me his role as the Spirit of the Deer in a dance he had created called *Legend*. I was grateful for the opportunity to perform with the company in a beautiful piece based on Indigenous spirituality. I had only a couple of quick rehearsals with David, and none with the entire cast, before I found myself thrust in performance into the middle of what felt like an ancient ritual, a vision quest set under, beside, and behind a huge, suspended, off-white wool macramé sculpture by Aiko Suzuki. I was surprised by the amount of physical energy I needed to harness for my solo with repeated jumps on one spot *en attitude*, arms lifted overhead, and fingers splayed like antlers. Breathless, uncannily alert, and wonderstruck by the dramatic lighting that threw evocative silhouettes from the set onto the stage, I wandered through a forest of light and shadow, encountering fellow spirits that suddenly materialized, expressed their essence, then vanished. It was a sublime experience.

The Canada Council grant to study abroad came through, and I was thrilled. Instead of using it for Israel, I decided to go to New York to study with Hawkins.

I called to say goodbye to Lisa, Terry, Mary, and the others, and Lisa asked me to come see her at their store for a chat.

"Why the fuck are you going?"

Lisa was a Scorpio; her questions, always intense, cut right to the point. Her gruffness could really turn people off. But not me. I tried to explain why I wanted to study with Hawkins, how his way of using the body was consonant with modern science and ancient spiritual practices.

"Why do you think your body is so important that it's worth all your time and energy focusing on it?"

"Uh, well, uh, I love to dance."

"But you're not going there to dance. You're looking for something more."

"Yeah, I guess so."

"You guess?"

"No, yes, I am."

"You know, when we went to Malaysia, we stopped in London and saw John Da Monte, a friend of Terry's, a healer whose intuition and wisdom Terry really respected. He asked me why I was travelling, if it was 'to see the world?' Not exactly, I said. I want to live somewhere where I'll be in the minority to experience what that feels like. And he said, as commendable as that was, there was no need for me to travel as I had everything I needed at home, and if I didn't have it but needed it, it would come to me."

I told Lisa how the Hawkins technique seemed to embody everything I was looking for and I didn't know of anyone practising it in Toronto. Besides, I wanted to go to the source. Lisa grabbed my hand.

"I just want you to remember this. If things don't turn out as you expect, look around and see what's really going on. Don't be so quick to blame yourself. Maybe it's not you."

Lisa's words were so kind and loving and she showed such genuine concern for my well-being that tears came to my eyes. I stood up and hugged her.

"Thank you. I won't forget."

                * * *

I ended up staying in New York for a year, and I found myself becoming a kind of personal assistant to Erick. He had a private room at the other end of his studio, which served as his personal office, library and, more often than not, bedroom. Sixty-three years old at the time, he was in great shape, not overly muscular but toned and fit, elegant in stature, intense, and self-assured in demeanour. He had an aquiline nose, dark, piercing eyes, and a full head of hair, not completely grey, that framed his chiselled head. He looked his name, kin to a hawk, Native American even.

One morning when I came in to make his coffee, Erick was in bed reading a translation of a classical Greek tragedy. He came across an unfamiliar word.

"Do you know what 'hake' means?"

"Uh, I think it's a kind of fish."

Erick looked it up in the dictionary he kept by his bed and sure enough, it was a kind of fish, related to the cod.

I don't know if this had been a test that earned me respect, but perhaps it garnered a little trust. He started to send me on errands, like buying big circular paper coffee filters in the West Village for his hourglass-shaped glass drip carafe. Tasked with buying him a pillow, I made a fool of myself in Macy's by pretending I had his large noble head and neck, while trying out various pillows for firmness and comfort. I didn't mind doing any of this for Erick, as I didn't have to pay for classes and was benefitting hugely from his teaching. I would be privy to his end of phone conversations with world-renowned sculptor and set designer Isamu Noguchi, be sent on errands to fetch something from the Chelsea loft of avant-garde artist Ralph Dorazio, or retrieve a prop from storage, having to move a large abstract expressionist canvas by Helen Frankenthaler to get at it.

In his classes, Erick loved to give illustrations with Zen koans or brief stories that highlighted some epiphany he had experienced, most having to do with how to live rather than explicitly how to dance. I fantasized that I was a student at Plato's Academy or an acolyte to an enlightened master. Erick would talk about the importance of eliminating conflict in one's life. He frequently quoted Krishnamurti, one of his favourites, just as Lisa often did.

"As Krishnamurti would say, 'If you want to be a thief, be a thief.'"

This I interpreted as, do what you want or need to do and do it fully, without ripping yourself apart about it. Do it without hesitation, judgment, or regret.

I also got to meet the inimitable, dynamic Lucia Dlugoszewski, his partner and composer. We would often meet for dinner at one of her favourite Japanese restaurants in the Village. She asked me to call her Lucy. She was short in stature, tending toward the zaftig, full head of thick, black hair, energetic — kind of like my mother at that age but she was nothing like my mother. Aside from being a revolutionary artist, she was funny and politically savvy. Watergate was slowly breaking in the news and she soaked it all up, thrilled that Nixon might finally be getting his comeuppance.

One evening, Erick and I took the subway to a music concert at Hunter College, possibly Alla Rakha on tabla, though I can't be sure. Erick despaired over the graffiti that defaced the subway cars and then went on a rant about the decadence of Andy Warhol and pop art.

"Putrid, all of it. You can smell the stench."

He sounded like one of the old guard, railing against contemporary crap, but I didn't disagree with him or the purity of his artistic vision.

As there were not many male dancers in those days, doors were opened to me that, were I female, I would have needed to be a much more seasoned dancer to be invited through. In the spring of 1973, I went on a U.S. tour with the Hawkins company, dancing in one of Erick's works. Cathy Ward, who had recently arrived in New York from Dallas, Texas, was a mentor, helping me prepare for the tour; she would, in later years, come to be the supreme embodiment of a Hawkins dancer. On the tour, I grew closer to company members Robert

Yohn, Beverly Brown, Nada Reagan, and Natalie Richman. Lucy and Erick were also on the tour as well as a small group of musicians. Erick always performed with live music, regardless of the expense.

I recall one sunny spring day when we were stuck in the theatre in a tech rehearsal that seemed to go on and on. There were problems with the lighting and the sound cues, so some of us left the theatre and went to a local greenspace to enjoy the spring day. I remember sitting next to a shrub and rubbing its twiggy branches and budding leaves against my cheek, blissfully feeling connected, with no separation between nature and me. That evening, Erick excoriated us for not remaining in the theatre. He said that to be a true artist, you needed to sit and listen with rapt attention, take every opportunity to learn your craft, and that included lighting. Perhaps excoriated is the wrong word. He was more rueful that none of us was tied to his side like an insatiable student patiently but eagerly soaking in whatever wisdom was available to further one's artistry, which, for Erick, was synonymous with one's life.

On the tour, I discovered that I had come to dislike performing. I loved the slowness, intensity, and camaraderie of dance training and class work, but performance was something else. I was so nervous onstage that all the strength would be sapped from my body, which was less than ideal for a dancer. Once, in a performance before a full theatre of over three thousand spectators at Indiana University, Bloomington, I lost my balance and fell. It's embarrassing and funny even now when I think of it. I was an angel with a stylized ladder on my back, touching Jacob as he dreamed, and as I bent over to touch him, I toppled over and wound up on the floor accompanied by the audience's ear-shattering, collective inhale.

Dancing in a piece I choreographed and performed for Lindy on her birthday, Winchester Street Theatre, 2017.

It wasn't long before I saw what my life would become as a professional dancer, and I didn't like the prospect. The dancer's world seemed too enclosed. Insular. Claustrophobic. I felt like there was a whole world that I was no longer part of. It seemed incestuous; dancers, as nice as they were, socialized almost exclusively with other dancers. I could not picture myself living with requisite periods on the road, the motels, hotels, lousy food, the darkness and unnatural light inside theatres, and the performances that were supposed to be the pinnacle and showcase of one's efforts but were less than satisfying.

Maybe a dancer's life required singular commitment and dedication that I was constitutionally incapable of mustering. This was not the life for me. I needed to break away. Would calling it quits mean that I had failed? Maybe I shouldn't be so quick to blame myself, as Lisa had told me. Maybe the artist's life was, by definition, self-centred and privileged, so removed from daily life that to give it up was to finally come to one's senses. Or was this just a loser's easy rationalization? Or, God forbid, maybe my parents were right and I should be doing something else.

When we got back to New York, I left Erick a note: "If you want to be a thief, be a thief. That is what I must be. Thank you for everything. Sam"

I returned to Canada.

11

Take Me Disappearing

MY FRIENDS ALVIN AND GLENNA HAD MOVED from the city with their daughter, Kael, and were now living in the Ottawa Valley. I went to stay with them and was welcomed back warmly. I dived into the life of a hippie farmer, planting crops in radiating sunray patterns that neighbouring farmers thought were idiotic, and baking blueberry pies with crusts that had more in common with fieldstone than food. Saturday mornings we'd go into Pembroke, the nearest town, and participate in the farmers' market, selling our organic produce to appreciative customers and bringing in a few dollars in exchange. As I contemplated my future, I'd dance in the fields and pay homage to the passing clouds.

I travelled to Toronto for my younger brother's wedding and stayed at Lisa and Terry's commune. Without my asking, they generously gave me the keys to the group's classic Mercedes to drive to the wedding, and the group en masse detailed it for me themselves until the windows, mirrors, chrome, and wood were restored to their original gleam. Understanding the value ascribed to image, they were excited that the luxury car could show my family on *its* terms that I wasn't a total hippie loser, even if I wasn't the doctor like Abie, or the lawyer Charlie, David, and Harvey were to become. I hardly looked the part of a Mercedes owner, wearing overalls custom-made out of Black Watch tartan with macramé rope suspenders, but this didn't seem to matter because the car worked its magic. Charlie even insisted on having his picture taken leaning against the car's sparkling grille, the brilliant Mercedes symbol front and centre.

At the wedding dinner, I danced with my mother, and she looked at me adoringly.

"Of all my children, you're my favourite."

"Please don't say that."

"Why?"

"It's not fair to my brothers, that's why. It's not right."

"It's the truth."

I knew she was being honest — I'd felt it many times while I was growing up: in her adoring comments about my eyes; in the frequency of her pinching my cheeks; in her consultations with me, not my brothers, on how she looked. But its expression in words made me uncomfortable, especially so at David's wedding. I wanted to explain further, to tell her about the psychological damage that parental favouritism caused, but her broad beam and the glide in her step made me realize the futility of the exercise. We continued to waltz.

* * *

A post-wedding discussion with Lisa about family politics was to lead to a dramatic change in the direction of my life.

"Why do people have children?" Lisa asked me.

"For the perpetuation of the human race," I answered half-jokingly.

Lisa continued to probe in her typical Socratic way. "Is it really the ultimate act of selflessness or is it something else?"

"I can't help think it's something else."

"Children are our route to immortality. We create a new human being in our likeness, part of us, a projection of us, insurance for our old age, a source of *naches* for us."

"You know that word?"

"It's the perfect word for what we're talking about. *Naches* is your payoff for raising children. That's the takeback. Your child is a reflection of you. Parents bask in their child's success as if it were their own."

"But in my parents' eyes, I'm a failure. I'm not doing what they want me to, yet my mother says I'm still the favourite."

"Sure. Prob'ly 'cause she knows you'll come around; it may take time, but you'll come around. There's nothing like the magic of a Jewish mother's guilt trip. If you don't make your parents proud, bring them *naches*, then what good are you? How can you be so ungrateful? Particularly if your parents are immigrants who worked hard, sacrificed the comfort of their lives so that yours could be better. And this dynamic intensifies a hundred times when your parents are Holocaust survivors."

"Hitler couldn't kill my mother, but I could."

"Yeah, get over that remark, already. I dare you."

By this time, I had slid off the couch in the living room and was sitting on the floor. Lisa came over and put her arms around me.

"I want you to hear something. It's from Dylan's *Bringing It All Back Home*. The second side is best listened to as a whole, but for now, Terry, why don't you put on 'It's Alright, Ma (I'm Only Bleeding)'?"

Terry located the album among the hundred or so on the shelf under the stereo. He pulled the disc out of its cover and examined it.

"Shit. This is the one that's all scratched."

"Next to the Lightnin' Hopkins album. The new one's there."

Terry found it, put it on the turntable, Side Two facing up, and placed the needle on the second last track. I had listened to this song many times, but had never heard it the way it sounded that day. I was knocked out by the rapid-fire poetry and wisdom of the words that had my mind spinning at 33 1/3 rpms.

I wanted to hear the whole of Side Two, beginning with "Mr. Tambourine Man," which is what we played once the requisite pot of coffee was made. Both Terry and Lisa knew all the words by heart and spoke/sang along with Bob.

Lisa picked up the thread of our discussion.

"So, who are you, if not a Chaiton? Are you a free and autonomous being or are you trapped, locked into an image of what your parents want you to be?"

I said that I thought I was free but also always felt like I was tied in knots.

"*Knots*, yeah —" said Terry, his voice rising with him. "That's the title of Ronnie Laing's latest book!" Terry had met R.D. Laing, the iconoclastic Scottish psychiatrist, while living in London in the sixties. "It's all about the double binds our families lay on us and then forbid us to even acknowledge, let alone confront."

"A family, by definition, values its own over anyone else's," continued Lisa. "Blood is thicker than water, you hear that over and over. But if you met your mother or father or brothers on the street and you didn't know them, would you want to be their friend? People say, 'I love them but I don't like them.' What kind of bullshit is that? But we are compelled to stay with our own."

"According to Laing," said Terry, "guilt is the glue that holds families together. To turn your back on your family is the worst crime in our culture. Anything can be forgiven, but not that."

Terry refilled our coffee mugs. Lisa lit up another cigarette, and I had one, too. She took a long sip of coffee. Her eyes, which were neither green nor brown, remained fixed on me, their laser focus seeming to dissipate the smoke in the room.

"I left home when I was fourteen," she said, turning her palms upward in a gesture not exactly of surrender but of having no choice. "My father, who was a dyed-in-the-wool Christian, wanted me to accept Jesus in my life and I couldn't do that. He said he wouldn't tolerate a daughter who didn't believe in Jesus living under his roof (some leaky roof!). So I left, hopped on a bus, and made my way to Toronto, luckily ran into someone I knew and built a life for myself. Was I better than the people I grew up with, the ones who stayed and lived the life their parents had forged for them? No. They couldn't leave; I couldn't stay."

"Did you ever see your father again?"

"Yeah, at his funeral."

"He never came looking for you?"

"As far as I know, he never changed...."

"Well, that's heavy."

"Identification is heavy," continued Lisa. "It creates a division between yourself and others when you have your religion, your family, your neighbourhood, your political party, your nationality. By definition, there's a greater value placed on being one thing rather than another; otherwise, why would you bother to identify yourself with anything?"

"But how can you not be what you are?" I asked.

"What you are? Okay, what are you?"

"I'm me."

"Right. And you're not me. That's what I'm talking about. If I'm Christian, then I'm not Jewish. If I'm Canadian, I'm not Tanzanian. If I'm a Chaiton, I'm not a Fitzgerald, and so on. It may not be that it makes you feel superior; it may make you feel inferior — or both. But there's a separation and a hierarchy built in that comes from the difference, all of it reinforced by imagery and repetition, by what we hear around us, what we read, see on television and the movies. It doesn't allow for the recognition of sameness, our common humanity or spirit or whatever you want to call it."

"I don't see that. Can't you be one thing and feel like you're equal to another thing? For example, being a woman and feeling equal to being a man?"

"Even that thought promotes duality, which leads to hierarchy. Why would I as a woman want to be equal to a man? Equal to what? To having a penis so you'll take what I say seriously? Equal to aggressiveness, coldness, disconnection from emotions, bossiness, a feeling of entitlement? Hell, no! Why would we want women to exhibit the same assholishness as men do? There's too much baggage that comes with it. We need to go beyond that."

"Is that even possible?"

"Well, according to Krishnamurti, when we examine our conditioning, we realize it's the basis of all conflict and

therefore war. We are at war with ourselves and that is manifested externally as war with the other."

"Now you've lost me."

"Okay. Let's find you. You were raised Jewish. That means
something."

"I don't think it meant that much in my life."

"Really? You don't have *a yiddishe kop*? Hasn't that been
drilled into you, that you're smarter than the *goyim*?"

"Uh, yeah, when you put it that way. But I don't take it
seriously."

"You don't? How do you know you don't?"

"I don't know. I know I don't consider myself Jewish in
terms of religion."

"Okay, well what about culturally? Look, you told me about
a number of your friends, and every time I asked you if they
were Jewish, you had to think about it and then give your answer, which without fail was 'yes.'"

"Yeah, it's kind of funny once you pointed it out."

"Funny, but not a coincidence. That's the same with all of
us. We're conditioned to stay with our own, Jews perhaps more
than most, out of pride (aren't Jews the Chosen People?) but
also out of fear: Who can understand us better? Who do we feel
most comfortable being around? Who can we trust? Who won't
harm us? The answer? Us, not them. But we don't acknowledge
that. We live our lives as if we're exercising free will, as if there's
a choice. But as Krishnamurti says, we're just images of something interacting with images of something else and not free
human beings."

Such was the tenor of our conversation, which went on
for many days as I revealed and examined every aspect of my
twenty-two-year life. I laughed in joy and sobbed in sorrow,

tried with the help of my dear friends to make sense of myself without the conditioned imagery that distorted everything and kept me from directly experiencing the world. I had always felt like an outsider — as a son, as a brother, as a Jew, as a Canadian — but still I had tried to be all those things and tried to belong. But, as Dylan said, it wasn't he or she or them or it that I belonged to. Who was I if I wasn't a Jewish man, Canadian, a Chaiton? What if these roles and images — the filters of me, us, them — were the source of my inner conflict? I could not claim to be a lover of peace if I was contributing to war. Not that I could personally end all conflict in the world, but if I could not end it within myself, what chance for the world was there? I realized that, without an internal revolution, the conflicts and divisions within myself would continue to be perpetuated in the external world. That recognition of personal responsibility hit me like a truck, shook me to the core, and the enormity of it made me cry.

Radical transformation was my only way forward. The last track of *Bringing It All Back Home* kept reverberating in my head, "It's All Over Now, Baby Blue." I needed to start anew, to shed the old, to let go. I was that vagabond rapping at my door, and I had to answer.

So I stayed and became part of the group. Lisa was right. It felt like home, like a home on steroids. Every day began with a feeling of excitement, possibility, and adventure; you didn't want to stray too far from the action out of fear of missing out. The fellowship, animated conversations, and energy electrified the house. There was coffee in the garden, tomatoes from the garden on toast, flowers from the garden, and the smoke of endless cigarettes and music, all punctuated by bouts of body-shaking laughter.

We made fun of one another in a way that would have seemed disrespectful to outsiders. It was intensely personal, yet no one took it personally. Terry the Virgo, forever caught up in detail, was laughed at for his inability to make up his mind, to see the forest for the trees. Lisa, the sharp-tongued Scorpio, whose tail could easily sting others as well as herself, was called "Oiseau" because she was actually soft and gentle as a little bird. We joked about her bowlegs (a result of rickets, when she was young and starving), her inability to add two and two together and come up with four (dyscalculia). I, the Libra, whose symbol is the scales, would be teased for my lack of balance or my obsession with art and beauty. "Pukeface" was one of my elegant nicknames that never failed to de-pompous me, to bring me down to earth. Eitel, the smiling ex-speed freak, was not only "Beaming" but also "the Junkie" and "the Nazi," with an uncle who had served in the SS, the Nazi paramilitary organization most responsible for the extermination of Jews, among others. An exceptional pastry chef and often in the kitchen, Eitel would grab me and pretend to stuff me in our gas oven. Insensitive and in bad taste? Yes, and a sacrilege, too. But what a way to face our fears, to neutralize our childhood demons (Holocaust iconography as well as fairy tales like "Hansel & Gretel") with humorous head-on assault.

Kathy, the "Finishing School girl," was mocked like Terry for being privileged. Gus, the alcoholic and wannabe Scot, was derided for his love of braying bagpipes. Mary, who easily mixed-up words, was nicknamed "Bumbles McJumbles." Bob, a superb gardener and cook, was "Bochas Rochas from Kalamazoo, Michigan," an American beauty queen. We all had nicknames that named our nicks, tore into the tribalism that separated us, and kept everything real.

My communal family, 1980. *Starting from the bottom, each step right to left*: Lesra, Lisa, me, Gus, Marty, Mary, Kathy, Terry, Eitel, and Eric.

We liked to say there were no rules to living in our house. Aside from Sundays when all of us would pitch in to do everybody's laundry and a major house clean up, there were no timetables or schedules for anything else, like grocery shopping, cooking, or washing dishes. Whoever was free and home at the time would shop if needed, would cook, and we'd all have dinner together, usually in the living room, plates balanced on our knees, eschewing the formality and familial ritualization of the dining room.

Rules were not really rules but arose naturally out of respect and care for one another. If someone was good at something, they did it with everyone else's support. No competition. No jealousy. Undemocratic in the sense that we didn't subscribe to the dictum that everybody could do everything equally. Nor was it a democracy where votes were taken and the majority ruled. Decisions were made by consensus, and on important issues, if consensus could not be reached through discussion, then no action would be taken. We lived together, worked together, laughed together — and all out of the same bank account. We shared all our resources, again not democratically but according to the socialist principle of "from each according to their ability, to each according to their need." It was also understood that if you wanted to leave, you left with whatever you came with.

We didn't fit the image of a commune with plentiful drugs and free sex. Alcohol and drugs were not tolerated. Eitel and Gus had recently stopped their drug-taking and drinking, respectively, and it didn't make sense to anyone else in the house to get stoned when they couldn't: to say, in effect, "Well, you can't drink or smoke up 'cause you can't handle it, but we can." It was a matter of solidarity and fairness. What we lost as individuals, we gained as a group, and the loss was illusory in any event. Similarly, while there were couples within the group, we did not sleep around with each other. After much debate, we came to the conclusion that free sex, although great in theory and wouldn't it be wonderful, was similar to drugs, like lighting a fuse on a bomb that could or would explode at any time. It was difficult enough for people to get along, for a group to be cohesive, without having one's brains scrambled or mood changed by external substances, without having to deal with personal jealousies and hurt that would inevitably arise with polyamorous relationships.

I loved this way of living, its consistency and lack of mood swings.

I started working at the Five Believers boutique. As the necessity arose, I learned how to do alterations on the clothing we sold; namely hems, which I sewed by hand. I wasn't particularly great at it but it felt like honest labour and made me feel like I was contributing to the group. There was something calming about it, too, and the irony of sewing did not escape me. I served customers, many of whom would come in just for the interesting discussions, loving the vibe, and would end up making purchases even though that was never the primary focus. We weren't making lots of money but it was enough for us to live on. Our lifestyle was comfortable, mainly because all our resources were shared. We were so much better off than if we lived separately, having to buy five or six cars, refrigerators, and sustain multiple, different households.

The cotton clothing we designed and sold was fine for Canadian summers, and what was called cruise wear. It became clear that to spread out sales year-round, a warmer location in the winter was necessary. Before I arrived, Terry, Lisa, and Bob had gone to Miami to scout for possibilities in South Florida. They stayed with Bob's aunt, who encouraged them to check out Palm Beach, where the moneyed crowd like the Kennedys vacationed in the winter. Palm Beach won them over with its intimate scale and gorgeous architecture and flora, and they rented a shop for the next season. Bob was American, and the American business would continue to be communal, but officially under his name.

I looked forward to getting away from Toronto and heading south. Before leaving, I wanted to say goodbye to my parents. I had come to realize there was no hope for change in my relationship with my biological family. My parents' expectations had continued to gnaw at me. I had no intention of studying medicine, of getting married, of having children. Whenever I was in their presence, I would look into their eyes and all I could see was disappointment. I needed to end the harm being done to myself and to them. The only way I saw out of this irreconcilable conflict was to absent myself from it. If I simply vanished, I'd be doing everyone a favour: releasing the knots that tied me up; sparing my parents my recalcitrance; sparing my brothers who did not need to see my mother, against all logic, favouring me.

It wasn't a churlish, spur-of-the-moment resolution but one that felt ethical and inevitable. At the time, and given the times, severing ties seemed not odd but natural. I was not bitter or angry. I was excited. Revolution was in the air, a complete break from the past more important than anything. It gave me a sense of relief, as if a great burden would finally be removed from my shoulders. I was living a new life, one that did not include my family of birth. I would tell my parents I was going to Florida, but I wouldn't tell them they would never see me again. Indeed, forever was not my intention. I was living in the present and the future was too far away to be concerned about. But I had made up my mind — I was going to disappear.

* * *

Steam rising from the sidewalk would no doubt have been visible in the searing rays of the setting sun had there been a sidewalk. But this being Wilson Avenue, like suburban streets of the time, sidewalks were urban ornaments that required shovelling or sweeping, and were better dispensed with altogether. There were, however, other indicators that revealed the heat of this late summer day, not least of them the sweat on my brow in the form of droplets that resisted dropping. It didn't help that I was wearing a sweater, but fear of revealing the mini-cassette tape recorder hidden in my shirt pocket argued against its removal.

As soon as I entered the vestibule of my parents' low-rise building, I remembered this was where my mother had carefully placed the five-foot benjamina tree I bought for her fiftieth birthday, a tropical tree in a drafty, north-facing window. That it didn't survive was no surprise. I reached under my sweater and switched on the recorder.

Why was I going to record my visit? As a memento? Something to replay if I ever got lonely or missed my parents too much or doubted the righteousness of my decision? That's not what I was thinking. The taping was the beginning of the covertness that was to characterize the next phase of my life. It was to be a window with a view to be shared with my friends, the people I had grown close to and felt a part of, a kind of devised family that, unlike my own, felt wholesome and true.

It was a ritual distancing from the bygone era of my childhood and youth, an artifact to be discarded after being listened to objectively with my new family.

I replayed the tape for my friends later, starting with the blare of the TV and my mother's piercing voice trying to coax from me what I wanted to eat. The icy clink against glass could be heard.

"Kool-Aid."

"Couldn't I just have some plain water?" The whine in my recorded voice made me cringe.

"Anything you want you can have...."

"Okay. Great."

"How about some chicken soup with *kreplach*, your favourite?"

"I'm not hungry."

"Look how skinny you are. You have to eat."

"I ate before I came."

"You want French toast?"

"Mom, I'm going away and I don't know when I'll be back."

"Away?"

"To Florida."

"Florida? Wait till it gets cold. We can go together."

"I'm going now ... moving there ... with friends."

"With who?"

"Friends! Terry, Lisa, Mary ... the people I'm living with, I'm in business with. You don't know them."

"Are they Jewish?"

"No."

"Don't go."

"It's no use you saying that. I just came to say goodbye."

"Who is going to take care of you if you get sick?"

"I don't know. They will."

"You can't trust them."

"Yes, I can."

"Don't go."

"I'm going."

"Wait a second. Turn up the TV."

"Mom, listen, can we just …"

"*The Sonny & Cher Show* is on."

"Fuck Sonny and Cher!"

"*Sha!* I want to hear this."

The sound of Sonny and Cher singing fill the tape, loud at first, then gradually fading as I went into the living room where I found my father in his boxer shorts, knee socks, and sleeveless undershirt, half-asleep on the plastic-covered loveseat.

"Dad!"

"Don't bother me."

"I'm going away."

"Please."

"I was wondering if you'd like to buy my stereo set. I can't take it with me and I know you always admired it. Cost me five hundred dollars. I'll let you have it for two fifty."

"What am I gonna do with it?"

"You'll listen. Connie Francis, Tzigan and Schumacher, whatever you want."

"I don't want it."

"How about two hundred? … Okay, I'll let it go for a hundred. It's already assembled. You don't even have to put it together."

That was the last time I would ever see them — my father dozing, my mother staring at the TV, eyes glazed over, neither of them present. I felt like I had already gone or, more accurately, that they were gone, had abandoned me, left me standing there alone. I was convinced that if my parents remembered me, it would be a fleeting reflection, an image that had nothing to do with the reality of me, and it wouldn't hurt them as much as it would hurt me to remain in their smothering purview. I had told my friends how prone to melodramatic emotional displays my mother was. The tape showed the brevity of her attention span, that her outbursts would be short-lived and fade into nothingness, just as I was about to do. At that moment in my life, I could not stay. And except for one postcard sent from abroad, I never got in touch with my parents again.

12

De Profundis

WE DROVE TO FLORIDA AND RENTED A HOUSE IN West Palm Beach, a typical two-storey construction with terra cotta roof tiles, a Florida room, Spanish wrought-iron railings on the staircase, and a large avocado tree in the backyard. Palm Beach was nestled on the other side of Lake Worth, across a bridge that used to have a welcome sign, like the ones on Toronto's beaches in the 1930s that read "No Jews and dogs allowed." The store Terry, Lisa, and Bob leased was located in the Via DiMario off Worth Avenue. Our landlord was a Jewish woman named Rose Edwards, who had been a dressmaker. For the obvious tribal reason, Rose was drawn to me and, of all my friends, could relate to me best. She would often invite me up alone to her apartment across the Via and feed me. Once, she gave me some homemade chicken soup to take away with the admonition that I just eat it myself and not share it with my friends. I took it home and promptly shared it with my friends.

Florida became the locus of my incipient political education. One of the first things Lisa wanted us to see was not the oceanside estates of the superwealthy, like the Kennedys or Marjorie Merriweather Post's (pre-Trump) Mar-a-Lago, but Belle Glade. One of the poorest areas in the United States, Belle Glade was where migrant farm workers lived in squalid bunkers, isolated and exploited for their labour, as Lisa had seen in the CBS documentary by Edward R. Murrow, called *Harvest of Shame*. Lisa was intensely alert to the needs of outsiders, those who had been marginalized and shut out. She never forgot where she came from, the hell of poverty she had lived in, the drunken violence of her childhood neighbours, although she was simultaneously aware, through her posh grandparents, of the lifestyle and values of the upper classes, which she could play into but was never seduced by. She had little patience for middle-class whining, for those who were oblivious to the privilege their white skin brought them. Every aspect of her life was devoted to the underdog, to righting inequality and injustice, to tipping the scales in any way she could. I needed and was grateful for the lessons she provided.

En route to Belle Glade (sounds like a Southern mansion, doesn't it? Something grand and pastoral that Scarlett O'Hara would have lived in), we had to keep our car windows closed. The air hung thick and yellow from the smoke of fires around Lake Okeechobee, where swamps were being burned off for land development. We stopped for gas and commented to an attendant about the foul air, and he didn't know what we were talking about. Although we couldn't see the sun in Belle Glade, we did see children, their hair in neat cornrows, playing outside on turquoise-painted concrete steps as if it were a bona fide playground in the Sunshine State. Belle Glade gave the impression of a slave labour camp, isolated from the rest of the world and with no apparent means of escape for its denizens. We felt fortunate to be able to leave.

On the way back, we stopped at a roadside shack where a white man was selling watermelons. He told us he would have more soon, but "you know how them donkeys is always late" with their deliveries. When we got back into the car, I said how amazed I was they still used donkeys, and Lisa quickly deflated my bucolic fantasy.

"'Darkies' not 'donkeys' is what he said."

Lisa, true to form, made it clear the vendor was slamming Black folks to us with a racist rant of how lazy and unreliable they were, taking it for granted that we white folks would understand and commiserate.

*   *   *

Across from our shop in the bougainvillea-bedecked Via was a store that sold Native American jewellery, crafts, rugs, and art. It was owned by a creepy white guy named Brian. Working for him was John Eagle Shield, a Hunkpapa Sioux from Standing Rock, who was extremely knowledgeable about Native American history and artifacts. In fact, he was just earning some income while on a mission to liberate sacred objects from museums around the country. He was especially intent on separating pipe bowls from their stems to release their spiritual energy, wherever they were displayed whole in gallery vitrines. A founding member of AIM, the American Indian Movement, he was at the occupation of Wounded Knee. He was also a feather and porcupine quill setter. This was one serious dude that we got to know well and love.

Brian was so obtuse that he did not know who he was dealing with. He wanted Eagle Shield to dress up and stand outside the shop wearing full regalia, arms crossed over his chest, silent and noble like a cigar-store Indian. When he refused, Brian suggested he put on a headdress and ride up and down Worth Avenue on a horse with a billboard advertising the shop. This suggestion did not pass muster either, or as Eagle Shield would say, "did not pass Custer." He had a great sense of humour.

We were fortunate that Eagle Shield trusted us enough ("You're not from around here, are you?") to educate us in Lakota and other First Nations' history and cultural practices. When we asked him about the scars on his chest, we learned about the sun dance and its huge significance in his life.

Often, he would call our home in the evening and would have long, intense conversations with Lisa about everything, including his own personal history and the abuse he suffered at the hands of white Mormon teachers who used to burn his wrists against hot radiators whenever he spoke Lakota, his native tongue. Once, Lisa asked him why he liked to talk on the phone so much, rather than come over and converse in person. He responded, "So I don't have to look at your white face and be reminded."

Brian was genuinely puzzled why Eagle Shield seemed so talkative with us but completely silent whenever Brian came around. The stunt he pulled with the turquoise and silver jewellery didn't help his cause. We used to get a fair number of famous people coming into our store, like Jose Ferrer, Celeste Holm, Mrs. E.I. Dupont, and the mother of playwright Edward Albee. One day, Elizabeth Taylor entered wearing a stunning, fine-woven wide-brimmed straw hat that Lisa admired and commented on. The celebrated actress removed her hat.

"Here, honey, why don't you try it on?"

They had a great time together, probably because Lisa treated her as casually but attentively as she would any customer. Eventually, "La Liz" left and disappeared down the Via toward Worth Avenue. This was just before the Academy Awards ceremony in 1974. A photo of Elizabeth Taylor wearing a Navajo squash blossom silver-and-turquoise necklace at an Oscar party was printed in newspapers around the world, including the *Palm Beach Times*. That picture soon appeared in the window of Brian's store with a handwritten message scrawled over it: "Loved the necklace, love Liz." The actress had not even gone into Brian's store, let alone purchased a necklace from him. Also, the handwriting, as Eagle Shield pointed out, was identical to Brian's.

* * *

We returned to Toronto in the spring, after the Palm Beach season was over. Not wanting to be found by my family, I continued to keep a low profile. This was not difficult since Toronto was a large and expansive city, then with a population of two million, and my brothers and parents stayed mostly in the northern part of the city, rarely venturing into my territory downtown.

Be that as it may, one day, a well-dressed woman walked into our Yorkville Avenue boutique looking for me. Ironically, our store was situated directly across the street from where I'd been born, in Toronto's original Mount Sinai Hospital at 100

Yorkville. I wasn't at Five Believers that day, but Kathy was. She recalls a short, square woman in a cream-coloured light wool coat, a bright scarf setting off her stiffly coiffed dyed blond hair.

"I'm Sam's mother."

Of course. Kathy knew that. She had heard my mother's thick Eastern European Jewish accent on the goodbye tape recording. Kathy steeled herself, frantically wondering what she was going to say to this woman who was so attached to her son that she could sniff out a lie in an instant.

"Where is he? I am looking for him."

Kathy honestly, and with impeccable Talmudic reasoning, said she didn't know where I was at the time. For all she knew, I could've been out shopping.

"If you see him, tell him a phone call wouldn't hurt."

Not long afterwards, I sent a postcard.

> *Dear Family,*
> *As you can see, I'm no longer in Florida. I want*
> *you not to worry about me. I decided to resume*
> *my dance career and am now performing with*
> *an avant-garde French company. We seem con-*
> *stantly to be touring around Europe. Enjoying*
> *it very much but the schedule is gruelling. Hope*
> *you are all well.*
> *Love,*
> *Sam*

There were three ten-centime stamps plastered along the top of the *carte postale*, each with a tiny likeness of Charles de Gaulle and a grand shot of the *tour Eiffel* on the front of the card that made its origin unmistakable. I had actually bought the blank card at a flea market in Florida, filled it out, and given it to a friend to mail from France, where he was going for the summer. I wasn't in France and I wasn't dancing. I just wanted to tell my family I was okay. I didn't want them to worry and I didn't want them to continue looking for me.

* * *

We carried on with the Toronto batik store through the seventies and had some success wholesaling to department stores across Canada such as Eaton's, Simpsons, The Bay, and Montreal's Ogilvy. We were able to put together a down payment on an incredible property on the Nordheimer Ravine just north of Casa Loma, outbidding a developer by just five thousand dollars. The house was one of those attractive plum brick Edwardian edifices designed by Eden Smith, like the Wychwood Library that I had admired as a child. It was full of light and flow, had a huge centre hall with a wide switchback staircase, a morning room, and a library with built-in walnut bookcases and a stone mantelpiece surrounding a woodburning fireplace.

Our social life continued to centre around our home, which we renovated ourselves, incorporating the butler's pantry into the kitchen, exposing a brick exterior wall, hand painting sprays of flowers on all the kitchen cupboards, and building a greenhouse extension onto the library. Digging into the overgrown garden, we unearthed stone walls and steps that descended into the wooded ravine we called the Hundred Acre Wood, after Winnie the Pooh's realm. We kept a huge compost pile at the back of the property and built a Japanese-style pagoda on the hilltop that afforded spectacular views over the garden and ravine. We rarely dined out, and only occasionally went to the movies. There was always so much going on around the house that it really didn't matter what we did. Just being together was unceasingly creative and fun.

*   *   *

In 1979, the second OPEC embargo hit, causing skyrocketing oil prices and worldwide shortages. By then we had grown tired of retail and were researching other business opportunities. We came across a British engineer who had invented a gas-saving device that, attached to a car's carburetor, reduced fuel consumption by 15 percent. At least that was the claim. Our interest was piqued but before investing, we needed scientific proof that it worked. To market this successfully, we also needed U.S. Environmental Protection Agency certification, and the nearest facility capable of testing and certifying was located in Brooklyn, New York.

It was in Brooklyn we met Lesra Martin, a fifteen-year-old African American who had been hired as part of a government-funded summer program for inner city youth, gaining work experience and earning some money to help out his family. Lesra was brimming with curiosity, warmth, and aliveness that met their best expression in his irrepressible grin. We made fast friends. Before long, we were introduced to most of his family: his father, Earl; Alma, his mother; sisters Noni, Lori, Starlene; younger brothers Elston, Leland, and Damon. Older brother Earl Jr., whom we didn't meet, had served time in prison and was seldom home. The family lived in a condemned four-storey building in the Bushwick section of Brooklyn, long before it became gentrified. Lesra's dream was that some day his family would get *into* the rat- and roach-infested, government-subsidized high-rise apartments that other families on welfare were trying to escape.

Lesra wanted to be a lawyer when he grew up. He had no idea what that entailed but he knew that lawyers got paid money when people were in trouble, and the people he knew were always in trouble. His older brother had already been to prison. At that time, one of every four African American men were under the control of the criminal justice system. Today it's one in three. It didn't take advanced math to figure Lesra's chances of needing a lawyer were much greater than his chances of becoming one. Lesra, we found out, was going into grade eleven and had placed third in his grade ten class. But for all intents and purposes, he couldn't read.

We invited him and a friend up to Toronto for the Caribana parade and we all had a great time. Soon, Earl Martin came up to visit and checked us out, and with his parents' permission and their desire for him to get a decent education, Lesra came to live with us. We homeschooled Lesra along with Marty, Lisa's son. I was their main tutor.

Lesra's literacy skills dramatically improved over the course of the next year, but not without struggle, courage, and a prodigious effort on his part. There was a huge distance to travel before Lesra would be able to follow his dream. Ultimately, he attended and graduated from Halifax's Dalhousie Law School. Today, he and his wife, Cheryl, also a lawyer, practise and maintain their own firm in Kamloops, B.C. They have two grown daughters, Brooklyn and Maxwell.

A milestone in Lesra's education — and in all our lives — was reached one brilliant late summer day in 1980 at a city-wide clearance of library books. To offset the whiteness of traditional Canadian learning materials at hand, we constantly looked out for books on African American history and culture. At the sale, we purchased a discarded hardcover copy of Rubin "Hurricane" Carter's autobiography, *The Sixteenth Round: From Number One Contender to Number 45472*. Lesra ended up reading the book out loud to us.

It was powerful and moving and made a convincing case for the Hurricane's innocence. In the racially charged period between the assassinations of Malcolm X and Dr. Martin Luther King, Jr., Carter was convicted of killing three white people in a Paterson, New Jersey, bar. We were aware this was not the first time in American history that a Black man had been railroaded into prison. Nor was it the first time in New Jersey history that an innocent man had been convicted of murder. We were reminded of Richard Hauptmann, who was executed in the infamous Lindbergh baby kidnapping case, about which we'd read a great deal.

Carter's graphic descriptions of life behind bars gave Lesra some sense of what it must have been like for his brother behind bars. Lesra now understood why Earl Jr., like virtually all prisoners, was close-mouthed about his prison experiences; no doubt because they were fraught with shame, too humiliating and too frightening to share even with — especially with — one's family. The connection for me here to my own family history, although not verbalized, was immediately apparent and filed away for later contemplation.

We wondered what had happened to the Hurricane after his book was published. I pointed Lesra to the acknowledgements section, which was dated September 1, 1973, at Rahway State Prison, New Jersey.

Doing the math, Lesra realized that was seven years ago. He was convinced that Rubin couldn't still be in Rahway, that he must have gotten out in the meantime because the miscarriage of justice was so evident. I told Lesra he needed to learn how to do research, especially if he wanted to become a lawyer. In those days, research could not be done online. You had to physically go to a library, consult card catalogues and librarians, retrieve books from the stacks, pull up old magazines and newspapers stored on microfilm and microfiche. We did this at the Metropolitan Toronto Reference Library.

Splashed on the front page of the *New York Times* were stories about the recantation of the state's two key witnesses, two petty criminals, who initially identified Carter and co-defendant John Artis at the scene. In 1974, the two key witnesses told journalist Selwyn Raab that their testimony had been coached, coerced, and bought by the prosecution in exchange for promises of reward money and leniency in the prosecution of their own crimes. Bob Dylan, after reading *The Sixteenth Round* and meeting with Rubin, wrote a song about the Hurricane and his case. There followed a huge outcry for justice, driven in part by a publicity campaign masterminded by the archetypal "Mad Man," George Lois, who had bumper stickers printed that said "There's only <u>one</u> innocent Hurricane!" Dylan took his tour, the Rolling Thunder Revue, to New Jersey and played at a women's prison where Rubin was being held at the time. There was an iconic fundraising event at Madison Square Garden with a video hookup and conversation between Rubin in prison and Muhammad Ali onstage, and where artists like Joni Mitchell, Robbie Robertson, Joan Baez, Roberta Flack, Allen Ginsberg, in addition to Dylan, performed. A similar event, "The Night of the Hurricane II," followed with The Who at the Houston Astrodome.

Before long, the Supreme Court of the State of New Jersey overturned the verdicts. New Jersey wasted little time in announcing they'd proceed with a retrial. Infuriated by all the negative publicity they had received from rock stars and New York "shysters," as they called Carter's pro bono lawyers, the prosecution really went for broke. They somehow got their star witness, Alfred Bello, to recant his recantation and once again say he saw the defendants with guns outside the bar just after the shootings. The prosecution also came up with a motive for the killings, where no motive was even offered at the first trial. Now the story was that Carter and co-defendant Artis supposedly heard that a Black bartender had been shot with a shotgun in a bar in Paterson earlier that night in June 1966, so they, in effect, appointed themselves avengers of the Black race and went into a white bar and killed the bartender and two patrons, also with a shotgun. Despite no evidence to support this "racial revenge" theory other than the fact the defendants were Black, it was allowed to be argued to the jury, and it was decisive. Carter and Artis were reconvicted and sent back to prison. The Passaic County Prosecutor told the press the guilty verdict "proved that a contest between an American jury and Madison Avenue hucksters is no contest."[4]

Silence descended. The uproar and celebrities faded away. Carter was confined to a five-by-seven-foot maximum security cell at Trenton State Prison, a penitentiary built in 1850. He kept to himself, reading and writing, still asserting his innocence: "I committed no crime. The crime was committed against me." He refused to participate in prison programs, refused even to go to the mess hall. His New York lawyers remained onboard and were pursuing an appeal.

We were shattered.

A few phone calls produced the Hurricane's Trenton State Prison mailing address. Lesra wrote the Hurricane a letter, his first to anyone. All of us wrote, too, thanking him for his engrossing book and for being such a strong and inspiring example of courage. Just a few weeks later, Rubin answered. Over the next months, more letters followed, then an in-person prison visit from Lesra, followed by collect phone calls to Toronto, which escalated into personal visits to Trenton from Terry, Lisa, Lesra, and me. Before we knew it, our family circle had grown.

In one of his letters, Rubin mentioned that his father had died just three weeks before Lesra's first visit. We encouraged him to write more about it, commenting on how powerless and alone he must have felt. We asked if he and his father had reached any kind of understanding. Rubin answered that he got to see his father the day before he succumbed to cancer. (Rubin's brother had to pay the state five hundred dollars for the privilege.) His father was no longer able to speak, but he was able to see, and what he saw was his son, handcuffed and shackled, escorted by armed guards into the hospital room. It was not a happy picture Rubin's father took to the grave with him, and Rubin wondered whether at some deep level he had wanted to hurt his father, to get some payback for his not being able to protect Rubin.

In retrospect, it also makes me question my relationship with my father. I wondered if my disappearing was, in some degree, similarly motivated, an attempt to hurt this man who had wounded me. But I wasn't thinking of my own history then and continued to distance myself from it. My brother Charlie, at my father's instigation, appeared one day at our door in the company of a police officer. My driver's licence had just been renewed, and Charlie pulled some strings and managed to get my Walmer Road, Toronto, address from the Ontario Ministry of Transportation. Terry answered and, following my instructions, denied knowing my whereabouts. I was hiding in our house library not ten feet away.

In August 1982, Rubin lost his appeal in the Supreme Court of the State of New Jersey in a four to three decision. As close as it was and even with a powerful written dissent, it was devastating. We had awakened in Rubin the hope that justice and freedom were imminent. Hope was now making it difficult for him to survive in prison. Each additional day behind bars felt like an eternity. We tried to buck him up, started to focus on getting his legal case away from the State, and to take the appeal federal. Rubin feared that the early details of the case, which excluded him as a suspect, were going to be lost to history. Taking that fear to heart, we all worked together full-time for many weeks, making a huge chart summarizing the evidence in his case and showing clearly that all evidence from the night of the crime exonerated Rubin: Just after the shooting, he was questioned, brought to the scene of the crime, was not identified by a survivor of the shooting, passed a lie-detector test, and was released. The press was told "he was not a suspect," and the grand jury heard the lead County Detective say that "the physical description of the two [gun]men is not even close [to Carter and Artis.]"[5] The state's case came into being over the next four months as records were altered and witnesses changed their stories. Rubin and John were then arrested and charged. The prosecution's case continued to improve over the ensuing years, as the chart made incontrovertibly clear.

We sent the chart to Myron Beldock, Rubin's principal counsel, and it buoyed him. All that was needed was an objective judge and a dispassionate review. Rubin was happy that he wasn't alone with the knowledge of the nefarious origins of the case against him. But his energy, in contrast to his usual exuberance, was flagging. What was the use? Madame Justice was blind, not in the sense of being impartial, but blind to the truth of a massively corrupt state and legal system. Rubin came to the decision he'd had enough. Resigning himself to life behind bars, he abruptly stopped calling.

The laughter and chatter along with the telephone's frequent ring that usually animated our house ceased and were supplanted by a deep and grieving silence. We were devastated by Rubin's withdrawal, especially at a time when we were building some new forward momentum. We had grown so close to Rubin, had shared his life so intensely that the abrupt loss of contact with him stung us to the quick. We could hardly speak about it.

Hindsight raises questions. Did I think that this is maybe how my parents and my brothers might have felt with my sudden vanishing? Bewilderment? An aching emptiness? A longing for contact, communication, some news, anything? A frantic hope that I was okay and safe? The parallel is obvious to me in retrospect, but I did not consider it at the time. As far as I was then concerned, Rubin's situation was sui generis. It wasn't a TKO, but the fight had been called, and the feeling in our corner was desolate.

13

Freeing the Hurricane

THE GAS-SAVING DEVICE THAT WE HAD TESTED in Brooklyn, although successful in helping us meet Lesra, did not perform well enough to warrant marketing. We launched a house renovation business instead and carried on with our lives.

Eight months passed before Rubin called Toronto again and we reconnected. He was entering his eighteenth year of unjust incarceration. But he didn't want to talk about himself. He was focused on some work we had begun together on the case of a fellow prisoner we called "The Rose," the title of a beautiful poem he had written. Several phone calls later, after we had completed writing The Rose's compelling submission to the court, the ice was broken. Rubin, speaking of himself now, told us he was ready. He was ready, he said, to let go of his chains. He was ready to be free.

We became single in purpose and resolved to go for broke. We were in for the long haul. We decided to split into two groups, put our beloved house up for sale, and find a rental. Lesra and Marty, now university students, were in the group that remained in Toronto and continued with our renovation business. They would support the second group, comprised of Terry, Lisa, and me, who moved down to New Jersey. Quixotic as it was, the goal was to get Rubin out of prison.

We spent the next three years conducting a new investigation into Rubin's case and working with his New York City attorneys: Myron Beldock, who was a well-respected civil rights lawyer and the son of a Brooklyn judge; and Leon Friedman, a constitutional law expert and Hofstra University professor. The way we worked together was the perfect expression of our ethos and the way we lived, and it was gratifying and validating when Rube's lawyers responded so naturally and enthusiastically to our group endeavour. With this attitude, we were able to charge ahead without doubts or fear clouding our vision. When asked, years later, why we did this, we'd always say, if your brother were wrongly incarcerated, wouldn't you do anything in your power to help free him?

At every turn, what we discovered reinforced our initial assessment of Rubin's innocence. We found a plethora of exonerating evidence: evidence of innocence, proof of prosecutorial misconduct, coercion of witnesses, suppression of exculpatory evidence, destruction and falsification of evidence, and the rampant racism that tainted everything. Simply put, the State's case was not unlike Hamlet's Denmark, rotten to its core.

Terry and I became expert in the massive record of the case — numbering in the tens of thousands of pages — that had gone on for two decades. We provided the lawyers with citations to trial and hearing transcripts, verified their accuracy, and wrote the factual portions of the habeas corpus petition that was submitted to the federal district court of New Jersey.

In hindsight, how ironic I was so eager to dive into this quest when I had assiduously avoided delving into my parents' history other than asking them questions. I never searched for documentary evidence, never read books or watched films about the Holocaust. Why? It was as if my parents' refusal to disclose was a bar against my going any further, as if not delving was a matter of respecting their wishes. Yet and still, I instinctively sensed I would have to go there, that I would go there eventually, when I got older, when the timing for me was right.

*   *   *

There was a special visit held in the prison yard that summer of 1985. The habe petition had been submitted and oral arguments heard in the federal district court. Judge H. Lee Sarokin's decision was pending. It was Family Day at Rahway State Prison, where Rubin was incarcerated. Sartorial, among other details, stand out for me. Rubin was wearing a light grey linen shirt with full, pleated sleeves and a Nehru collar designed by Willi Smith; Lisa had on a brilliant white Ralph Lauren peasant blouse and matching full-length skirt. The sun graced the occasion with its warming presence and the sky offered azure clarity softened by the occasional white puff of cloud. We sat in a circle. Terry was there, too, and The Rose as well as some other of Rube's prisoner friends that we had gotten to know. One of them was a barber who cut Rube's hair and we called him "Shakey." There was much teasing and laughter, and like a plein-air picnic with genial companions, the feeling was *gemütlich*.

I remember smiling, leaning back in my plastic chair, and dreamily looking up toward the sky. But at that moment, I saw only the fourteen-foot walls and towers flanking the yard and in the towers the guards with guns. And I noted the barbed wire running across the top of the walls and the huge steel doors that separated the yard from the pond with the Canada geese on the other side. And for the first time, I felt like I was in a concentration camp, that I'd gone through a portal and was transported back in time to a concentration camp on a mission to liberate my parents — the dream of every Holocaust survivor's child.

* * *

One day in early August, on a break from writing a Reply submission to the State of New Jersey's demonstrably false and stale arguments to Judge Sarokin, I was sitting on the toilet in the small generic bathroom in our Rahway apartment. I was feeling a little dizzy with all the hopscotching through various briefs, and I thought I heard my mother's voice. She was calling my name. "Semele, Semele, Semele." I heard it several times. But then I questioned myself, wondering if my fatigue and the sound of the toilet flushing were playing tricks on me. I thought nothing more of it — until, a few weeks later, when Kathy returned to Rahway from Toronto.

After Oral Argument in Judge Sarokin's court, Kathy went back to Toronto for some medical appointments. An article in a local newspaper caught her attention, about a car accident on Highway 11 in cottage country. An older couple, both survivors of the Holocaust, were alone in their car when it crashed. Luba Chaiton died at the scene and her husband, Ralph, succumbed later to his injuries. Kathy waited to give me the awful news in person.

And I didn't cry.

I didn't feel anything except a kind of numbness. My mother and father were gone? I couldn't help thinking, What an ordeal life is! Hitler didn't kill them. I didn't kill them. A car crash took their lives. Weren't they once involved in a car accident and called home from the hospital in the middle of the night? Did I remember that correctly or was it a premonition of what was to come so many years later? How could this have happened again? A déjà vu? No, it couldn't be a déjà vu because the outcome was different. This was it, then. The end? For real? My mind was racing, dulling my senses.

It took me some time to process the news. I'm still processing. Did I regret my self-imposed estrangement from my family? Did I regret the course my life had taken? I asked myself then and I ask it again now.

I was at a loss — what to say, how to feel. That night, a dreamless sleep gave me no succor, filled in no blanks.

The next day, while driving on the New Jersey Turnpike on our way to Beldock's office, Kathy and I talked. She spoke of the emotional estrangement from her own mother, how difficult it was to reconcile. I said I was grateful that my mother had loved me as much as she did. Kathy was surprised, given my avoidance of my mother and how I'd felt smothered by her. Yes, all that was true, too. But however inadequate it had been, I wondered if there was some strength, some sense of self-worth that my mother's crazy love had engendered in me, something that could never be taken away, even though she was now gone.

My dad? I don't know. Gone, too, but was he ever really there? Not for me. We were never close and I never really liked him.

I needed to bury the hope I'd carried all those years, the expectation that one day my mother and father would be willing and able to bare their souls, to reveal themselves to me. With their deaths, the possibility of rapprochement had been taken away. The possibility of learning who they were, finding out their stories, of them learning who I was and had become — all was gone. It wasn't total numbness but a finality that I felt, an abandoned mid-chapter of a book that would never be written, that I would never read or get to write. Maybe it was a tale they didn't need to tell, a story I didn't need to know because if I needed it, it would have somehow manifested itself to me. Anyway, there were no more kicks at this can. Or so I thought.

Why, I now ask, didn't I cry? Why didn't I rush back to Toronto, reach out to my brothers, visit my parents' graves? If not when I was working on Rubin's case at a critical stage, but later when it had been resolved? Why, indeed. I had so thoroughly divorced myself from my blood family that they'd already been erased from the world I was living in and ceased to exist for me. Without realizing it, I was part of a Jewish tradition in which a parent, like Tevye the Dairyman in the Sholem Aleichem story, who pronounced one of his daughters dead to him when she decided to marry a non-Jew. If a Jewish parent can excommunicate their offspring, the reverse can also hold true. I had cried long and hard about it in that conversation so many years before with Lisa and Terry, when I realized that to free myself from conflict, nothing short of a personal revolution in my life was necessary. I had gone on to create a new life, to erase myself from my parents' purview, to orphan myself long before death had taken them.

I needed to focus on Rubin's liberation; on life, not death; on the future, not the past. Call my brothers? I didn't seriously consider it. That life was over. Now that my parents were gone, there was nothing except our surname tying us together.

* * *

On November 7, 1985, Judge Sarokin's decision dropped in the media worldwide, like a bolt out of the blue:

> The extensive record clearly demonstrates that petitioners' convictions were predicated upon an appeal to racism rather than reason, and concealment of evidence rather than disclosure.
>
> The jury was permitted to draw inferences of guilt based solely upon the race of the [defendants], but yet was denied information which may have supported their claims of innocence. To permit convictions to stand which have as their foundation appeals to racial prejudice and the withholding of evidence critical to the defense, is to commit a violation of the Constitution as heinous as the crimes for which these [defendants] were tried and convicted.[6]

Judge Sarokin ruled that Rubin's conviction, which "rests upon racial stereotypes, fears and prejudices," was such a violation of fundamental rights that "the court will grant the writ...."[7]

The reversal was huge news, nationally and internationally. The story was at the top of the front page of the next day's *New York Times*, and Rubin's picture was to be on the front page of Canada's *Globe and Mail*.

In the federal court the next day, the prosecution declared its intention to appeal the judge's decision and argued that Mr. Carter should not be released pending that appeal. He was a danger to the community, they argued. When asked to point to any recent evidence to show what risk he posed, the prosecution could find none. Judge Sarokin took a brief recess to consider the matter, then issued a ruling: "I cannot, in the face of the conclusions reached in my opinion and the injustices found, permit Mr. Carter to spend another day or even an hour in prison, particularly considering that he has spent almost twenty years in confinement, based ... upon a conviction which I have found to be so constitutionally faulty.... Mr. Carter's past imprisonment may have been a travesty. To continue it would even be a greater one...."[8]

The judge looked up and focused directly on Rubin.

"I am confident that Mr. Carter will not disappoint this court or all those persons who believe in him."

The jammed courtroom erupted in shouting, applauding, cheering. David had slain Goliath! Rubin's friends, lawyers and supporters, boxing fans, photographers, journalists — all of us went crazy with joy, as did prisoners and even some prison guards, we later learned. As the throng spilled noisily out of the courtroom onto the sidewalk outside, newsroom helicopters hovered overhead. Through a side door, Rubin made his thrilling escape. It gave prisoners not only in Rahway but around the world the hope that justice is indeed possible; that triumph over the defeat and despair of their lives is attainable;

that perseverance in the face of monumental oppression and unjust persecution can, in the long run, set things right.

We were expecting to head immediately back to Canada with Rubin. Our apartment in Rahway had been packed up, Air Canada reservations had been confirmed. We were ready to leave. Frantic, joyful preparations had been made by our group in Toronto, a house in Rosedale rented, flowers placed everywhere, the fridge filled with Rubin's favourite foods.

But it was not to be — not yet. The State of New Jersey was rabid in its appeal of the Hurricane's celebrated release from prison. Two and a half more agonizing years of continuing to fight the prosecution lay ahead. At least Rubin was at liberty, even if he could not leave the country because of the State's ongoing obsessive persecution.

For the first year, we all (Rubin and the Canadians) lived together in New York City. When it looked like the appeal was going to drag on for years, we decided to find a house in the country where we could keep two horses we rescued from a hack barn in the Bronx. We rented an upscale colonial clapboard house in Westchester County less than an hour north of New York City in Bedford where, for the benefit of the horsey set, broad sandy trails meandered through the woods and the roads were left unpaved. It was in the Bedford house that Carter and Partners, as we had dubbed our "law firm," worked along with Beldock and Friedman on the brief to the Third Circuit Court of Appeals, reviewing once again the mammoth record of the most litigated prosecution in New Jersey history. The stakes were high: the Hurricane's newfound freedom hung in the balance.

Day after day, the dining room table was strewn with yellow legal pads, the floor a tumble of briefs and transcripts

fastened with metal grommets. One of those days, I recall
feeling particularly overwrought. Needing a cigarette break,
I went into the living room and lit up. The view through the
window provided a calming distraction. Fog that had obscured
the woods to the northeast was slowly dissipating. I noticed,
behind a birch sapling, a spectral shape gradually materializing.
First there was a chest, then legs, a neck, and ears, body parts
coalescing in the form of a white-tailed deer — silent, delicate
but alert, present where there had been absence. And the moment I blinked, it was gone.

I marvelled at the deer's cleverness in camouflage and
stealth, at its ability to hide in plain sight, to appear and disappear seemingly at will. What I had witnessed, I realized, was
a natural survival technique, and a feeling of kinship with the
deer overtook me. I, too, had hidden in plain sight in a bid for
self-preservation. I thought about the blood family I had left so
many years before, about my parents who were now gone. Was
the deer showing me that nothing really disappears?

I had quit smoking by the time the Third Circuit appeals
panel unanimously upheld Judge Sarokin's ruling and his
grant of the writ of habeas corpus. Rubin won another round,
a major round. True to form, the prosecution filed its Petition
for Certiorari to have its appeal heard in the U.S. Supreme
Court. Carter and Partners were called to the bar once again
on the facts and Professor Friedman wrote the legal portions of
our Brief in Opposition.

On January 11, 1988, the U.S. Supreme Court refused to
hear the State's appeal. This meant that the highest court in the
land had decided Judge Sarokin's decision was correct and ab-
solutely final. Rubin had won this championship fight, but the
victory was tinged with a bittersweetness. I see him sitting in a

comfortable old leather armchair in Bedford, the sun streaming through the window on this brilliant winter day. Beldock had just given him the news. Lisa, Terry, and I — all of us — could barely contain ourselves, and we were whooping and hollering and jumping up and down in triumph. But Rubin grew suddenly melancholic. The phone receiver he usually held tight up against the side of his head, his biceps flexed, dropped to his lap. He looked over to Lisa, Terry, and me, rejoicing in the room, and quietly said, "You stole my march."

The State of New Jersey had the option to retry Rubin for a third time. The original indictment, "Passaic County Indictment No. 167-66, charging defendants Rubin Carter and John Artis with Murder in three counts," was still valid. Rubin's New Jersey attorneys had calls and meetings with various members of the New Jersey Attorney General's Office, asking that they step in and quash further proceedings. They claimed their hands were tied; the decision rested with the Passaic County Prosecutor's Office that had issued the indictment.

After much discussion, we decided to pay a visit to Frank Xavier Graves, the mayor of Paterson, who had also been the mayor in 1966, when the murders Rubin was convicted for occurred. Our research into Rube's case led us to conclude the murders were actually part of a mob war where various families were fighting over territory. We'd always believed Graves was like a mob boss, or did the bidding of the mob bosses in Passaic County, and we had no doubt he was pulling strings back then. Rubin recalled news conferences the mayor had given, trying to quell the public's anxiety about these killings. Mayor Graves had called the homicides "one of the most heinous crimes" in the city's history and ordered nearly one third of the city's police force to be marshalled to the investigation.[9]

One of Rubin's New Jersey attorneys, the brilliant and fearless William Perkins, a Black lawyer from Jersey City, would accompany Rubin, Beldock, and me to see Mayor Graves. We thought it was worth a shot.

I was scared shitless as we approached the Headquarters for the Department of Public Safety in Paterson, where Mayor Graves, along with his Police Department, was hunkered in a concrete bunker of an edifice that looked like how I imagined the Ministry of Love from *1984*. Rube and I felt a modicum of protection from Beldock and Perkins and the extraordinary press coverage the vacation of his convictions had engendered. But this was Paterson, enemy territory, where, history had taught us, anything could happen.

As soon as we traversed the building's entrance, we were frisked and put through metal detectors, then ushered into a tiny elevator to the third floor where interrogation rooms were located along with the mayor's office. Exiting the elevator, we came up against two bulky toughs who flanked the mayor's doorway like armed fu dog lions. They immediately popped out of their chairs, and I was surprised at how short they were, even in Cuban heels. They excitedly greeted Rubin, as if he were a movie star. They knew him back in the day when they'd attended the same public school together. Rubin remembered them and laughed.

They escorted us into Mayor Graves's office, then abruptly took their positions in the shadows at the rear of the cavernous room. We felt like Bonasera entering the godfather's dark den on his daughter's wedding day to ask a favour of the godfather. Graves got up and walked around his huge desk. He shook Rubin's hand and offered his congratulations.

"Well, you made it, buddy."

They joked about Rubin still being in fighting shape and asked when he would be making his comeback. They reminisced about different people they knew in common, mostly police officers, some of whom were still working in Paterson.

"So what can I do for you?"

Bill Perkins took the lead. "Mayor, we'd like you to exert your influence as an elder statesman, for the benefit of all parties. We're trying to lay this whole thing to rest and not have the Passaic County Prosecutor's Office pursue a third trial."

Myron Beldock emphasized that the prosecution's case had been completely demolished and discredited.

Graves shrugged. "What can I say? Mr. Carter's still standing after all these years. He won fair and square. There is no good reason why this thing should keep going on. But what can I do? The decision is not mine to make."

Not long after the mayor's pronouncement, a Passaic County judge signed an order dismissing the twenty-two-year-old indictments.[10] The sixteenth round was finally over, and the Hurricane was free to go.

After Rubin's appearance the next morning on ABC's *Good Morning America*, Rubin, Terry, and I jumped into our car and headed north to Canada. I'm not sure we stopped even once before reaching the border. We didn't want to press our luck.

It was humbling to realize what was possible when people work together unselfishly. The magnitude and beauty of our victory would be celebrated for years to come. No one involved was left untouched by the experience, and this feeling extended to Judge Sarokin as well. He has stated on many occasions that freeing Rubin "Hurricane" Carter was the most rewarding action he had taken in his tenure on the bench: "There's no greater or more important thing a judge can do than free the innocent."[11]

14

Reappearing

A QUADRENNIAL LEAP YEAR DAY MARKED OUR arrival back in Canada in 1988. Returning home from a foreign war is rarely an easy adjustment for combatants. As victorious as we'd been, we felt drained, exhausted, enervated. Rubin underwent his own kind of stress, not knowing where he stood, his personal liberty still fresh and odd — odder still in Canada — after so many years of incarceration in the Land of the Free.

Toronto seemed different to me. While we were away in the trenches, the untempered greed of the 1980s had exploded into a plethora of BMWs crowding the roads and mind-boggling varieties of mustard and balsamic vinegars packing grocery shelves. The city thrummed with traffic, manic energy, and new riches. But at its heart, I was conscious of a silence. An absence. A lack.

After his release, Rubin Carter lived with us on and off for nine years until 1994. He had been great in prison, beyond great in fact. His ability to maintain dignity and integrity in that most inhospitable of environments was a mind-boggling achievement. There, as I've said, he was at home. His low prisoner number was a badge of honour (by the time he was released, new numbering had hit the ninety thousand range). He knew the rules, which ones he could break, which were inviolable. He had the well-earned respect of virtually every group inside, from the mafia wise guys to the Black Muslims, to the bikers, white power advocates, and the guards. He was open, generous, knew how to keep the peace. He mentored and protected younger prisoners like The Rose; he shared precious books with them, had ongoing philosophical prison-yard discussions, encouraged them to examine their lives, to question everything.

We thought that, once out, Rubin would write a new autobiography that would tell the story of his journey from #45472 to liberated man, free both physically and spiritually. It would also be an indictment of the death penalty and the prison industrial complex. He planned to call it *No Holds Barred, No Bars to Hold*, and its opening line would be, "I disappeared from prison long before they let me go."

In a house we rented just north of Toronto, Rubin was furnished with a new IBM PC, a quiet space in which to write, and plenty of coffee. What we couldn't provide him was the ability, at this point in his life, to focus. He could not bring himself to write about how he finally was able to get out of prison; instead, he busied himself with rehashing old war stories about prison riots and his friendship with a particular federal marshal. Still, we managed to cobble together a proposal that we sent to Leon

Friedman, who had stellar contacts among the publishing elite in New York City and would act as Rubin's agent.

As famous as the Hurricane was, no one jumped on the book. Some loved the story but wanted to hire a professional journalist to write it. Rubin didn't want to cede control of his life story, and as much as we were all counting on funds from a book to live on since our finances were depleted, we didn't want to go there either. But that was all moot, anyway.

Once the prison doors were opened, Rubin was lost. We'd had a hint of this when Beldock told him the news that the Supreme Court would not hear the State's appeal. Rubin, who was finally free, looked deflated and accused us of stealing "his march." Rubin's sense that his identity as a wrongly convicted man had been taken away from him was a moment of an unexpected truth that we found shocking. Did we do this to him? Hadn't we all worked together for a common goal — his freedom? Wasn't this what he said he wanted? We decided we couldn't take it personally. It was Rubin's fear speaking. What was he going to do now? Who was he going to be? His entire being, so it seemed, had been invested in his innocent-man-in-a-living-hell stance. This turmoil was an augur of what Vern Harper, a Cree elder we were to become close to, was to say is common wisdom among First Nations' people, "The day you get out of prison is the day your sentence begins."

Vern knew whereof he spoke, having himself been a former boxer who, out of reverence for Carter, had adopted the name Hurricane and also served time in prison. Rubin now didn't know his place, neither in Canada nor in the world. He tried to eke a tinge of control by focusing on the familiar. Like checking and rechecking all the doors in our house to make sure they were secure when we went to bed. In order to sleep, he

needed to be locked in. But this was not something he wanted to discuss. Whenever we brought up his prison experience,
encouraging him to speak about it, he would become resentful
and shut down. Why were we always throwing it back in his
face? Couldn't we allow him to just put this shit behind him
and move on?

Rubin was ostensibly a fifty-year-old man, but in reality,
he was in his twenties, frozen, like other prisoners, at the age
his freedom was taken from him. Released from prison, he was
suddenly a young man who could suffer no constraints. He saw
everyone — not just those who tried to guide or counsel him,
but anyone who touched him — as a prison guard. On New
Year's Eve in 1988, in a small ceremony in our house north of
Toronto, he married Lisa. Their theme song was "I Want to
Know What Love Is" by Foreigner. Lisa's love was total and un-
conditional. In Rube's mind, however, their marriage changed
little except his legal status, allowing him to remain in Canada.
For him, calling the wife "the old ball and chain" was not a
joke. He loved how we had worked together to get him out of
prison but he didn't or couldn't love the togetherness once out.

So how was the Hurricane going to survive? We felt it incum-
bent on us to help him replace his prison identity, his "march,"
with something he could be equally proud of. He was an extraordinarily dynamic and charismatic public speaker, in the tradition of Southern preachers, and so we helped him launch a new
career. Terry and I wrote his speeches and arranged speaking
engagements for him across Canada and the U.S. at universities,
legal conferences, and forums. His speaking fee rose steadily and,
at first, all went smoothly. But every once in a while, when he felt
overwhelmed, he would jump in his red Jeep, drive back to New
Jersey, where he would party, and feel free.

What were we to do? How were we going to survive? I stepped forward and said Terry and I should write the book. After all, we knew the story. We were part of it. We had honed our writing and narrative skills in our work on the briefs. We'd kept my phone call notebooks, our investigative notes, Rubin's legal papers, briefs, transcripts. So that's how we came to write *Lazarus and the Hurricane: The Untold Story of the Freeing of Rubin "Hurricane" Carter*. It was an intense, cathartic, sustained effort, requiring over a year of full-time work.

Doing publicity for the book was how I was discovered by my blood family. After I appeared on a national news magazine show, *The Fifth Estate*, Canada's version of *60 Minutes*, Abe (no longer Abie) left a message at Penguin Canada, our publisher. Our editor, Iris Tupholme, called him back and was shaken by the quaver in his voice.

"You don't understand. We thought he was dead."

Abe explained that the family had not seen me in nearly twenty years, had no idea if I was even still alive.

I got the message, bit the bullet, and returned Abe's call. His voice sounded like mine; mine, his.

"Yes," I said, "I'll come and we can talk."

My disappearance had come to an end.

Being in the public eye, I expected this discovery to happen; indeed, I must have wanted it to happen. I had kept my name, never seriously considered changing it. It was an essence that could not be jettisoned, an unbreakable thread that pulled me back to my origins and the unfinished business demanding resolution. And yet, as I parked on my brother's midtown Toronto street, I had to force myself not to shift into reverse and vanish again.

I turned off the ignition, but my mind remained in gear. Here I was, the prodigal son returning home. Would a celebrated achievement be enough to offset my family's hurt and anger at my sudden disappearance? Would it suffice as a cause for *naches* even if to see me again after nearly two decades of invisibility might be a great shock?

I got out of the car and closed the door, raised my eyes, and steadied myself. As if unstuck in time, I traversed the liminal space. Moving along a tulip-flanked path, up three flagstone steps to the front door of an elegant Georgian house. Thinking my brother, the doctor, has done well for himself. Wondering if my other three brothers have already arrived. Half-expecting shouting, rancour, tears. Thinking about the deer that disappeared four years earlier, about my parents who had disappeared six years earlier. Thinking about the Mothers of the Plaza de Mayo (a disproportionate number of them Jewish) who mourned the *desaparecidos*, their adult children who had been disappeared by the Argentinian military junta. Thinking about myself who left voluntarily eighteen years ago. Why did I disappear? And who was it or what was it that disappeared? Was it self-preservation or liberation? Extinguishment and nullification as a road to transformation? Can anything in our universe truly disappear or does the First Law of Thermodynamics, the Law of Conservation of Energy, always hold? Does the energy remain and just shift, taking shape in surprising forms, like the deer in Westchester? I was spinning out, apprehensive about the impending clash of forms, about my reception and the cognitive dissonance in having my old and new identities simultaneously appear.

I rang the bell and chimes filled my ears.

Abe opened the door. He took a moment to look me up and down, then hugged me warmly. He was still a few inches shorter than I was, but instead of hair, a shaved pate beamed up at me. He led me into an open living room, a dazzling skylit space, the sun streaming on a solid pine hutch featuring framed family photographs, including one of my parents looking older than I'd ever seen them, more like someone's grandparents than the parents I once knew.

Abe's two grown children, Josh and Dana, hovered in the background, trying to stay out of the way but riveted to the scene. I had last set eyes on Josh at his bris. Now, in 1991, he was twenty and, as before, close to tears. My niece Dana, a self-possessed young woman, I'd never met. Nephew and niece — I marvel at the words. I had lived most of my life communally with friends. Blood relationships had become alien to me and still today necessitate conscious effort on my part to verify that I've used the appropriate term. "How should I refer to your son?" I recently asked Dana. "My great nephew?"

I had a chance to speak with Abe before brothers Charlie (from that moment, I would hear him only called Charles) and Harvey arrived. Abe outlined his considerable efforts in trying to find me over the previous two decades. I thanked him for his care and concern but did not explain why I had vanished. I had been determined to avoid contact, and didn't, even then, tell him how close Charles had once come.

Abe looked at me with a combination of weariness and pity. "You know, of course, about Mom and Dad?"

I didn't know the details, I said, but I wanted to.

Mom and Dad were driving north up to Abe's Muskoka cottage for a long summer weekend in 1985. En route, our father had a heart attack. Our mother leaned over to grab the steering wheel, but it was too late. Their car crossed the median and struck an oncoming truck. Mom died almost instantly from a fatal head injury; Dad regained consciousness after being ambulanced to hospital.

"Where's Mommy?" Dad asked, and neither Abe nor Charles, who were present, would answer. Mercifully, our father never found out — he went into a coma from which he never emerged.

Abe had to identify the body of our mother. As he approached the table in the morgue, he noticed an arm uncovered. He didn't need to look at her face. Her tattoo was a dead giveaway. This picture he will never be able to erase from his mind, nor I from mine, and the hush and tentative gait of his voice told me that was all he wanted to say about it.

But there was more to say and I would say it in a poem I was to write years later:

Inventory

Blue ink on
pale flesh
I see the number
now
on inside forearms
left and right
I can't remember which
Although I know it must have been
Only one.
There was, I think, a letter too
And a dash followed
By five or was it
six, maybe seven, digits?
I can't remember.
Yet it is not time

That dims my memory
But your shame.
You never wanted me
To see
And I didn't
out of respect
I didn't
see
Because you were
My mother.
Not a slave, a cow,
a dog
with a tattooed
number.
You were my mother.

Abe continued his wrenching recitation. He told me about having to remove my parents' belongings from the wrecked car, its trunk laden with food. He picked up a bakery box full of goodies Mom had brought as a gift, a tidy white carton secured neatly in four directions with white string finished in a bow. He pulled at the bow and flipped open the lid. Of course, there were blueberry buns in the box, it being early August and the height of blueberry season. The memory, six years later, brought him to tears, and did the same for me.

"I froze Mom's blueberry buns and ate them all slowly over several months, one by one, trying to drag out my last tangible connection to her.

"Dad lived four weeks before he passed. He was alert for the first two weeks and we thought he might survive. But then his heart, kidneys, and lungs gave out. We finally elected to turn off the respirator when he was found to be brain-dead. We [four brothers] were all at the bedside as the switch was turned off. We watched his colour and life fade away."

David later told me that he completely broke down at that point. He was convinced Ralph would recover, and was prepared to have him come live at his house. Overwhelmed, David exited the hospital room and found Uncle Yankel in the hallway. As distraught as Yankel was by the passing of his oldest brother, he insisted David get hold of himself.

"You must stop crying!"

Yankel, as if his own life depended on it, was a master at stoicism. David was not.

Abe had tried desperately to find me after the car crash. The search was frantic. Had they looked in Rahway, New Jersey, they would have located me. As Abe spoke, I realized that my mother's voice had found me there: "Semele, Semele, Semele." It must have been at the moment of her death that she called out to me. The timing was exact. Oh my God. What did that mean? Her final adieu? That she was reaching out to me then — and my hearing her — made me think how connected we were to each other, even after all the years I'd been gone. And I felt enormous guilt.

Charles and Harvey arrived. Although they hugged me, I sensed their conflicting emotions, their reticence and mistrust as well as their relief that I was alive. Nothing I said cut it for them, although they didn't say so. It had been abandonment, plain and simple. Even if I were the prodigal son, I was returning to the glare and approbation of the media and not to them personally, which only made them angrier. How could I have devoted so much time and energy to doing good for a stranger when I had neglected my own? Was I oblivious to the tribulation my disappearance had caused the family? I was nowhere to be found even when our parents died! David, the sibling I had been closest to, couldn't forgive me and didn't show up that day. It would be a long time before we saw each other.

More details were filled in. It wasn't long after the accident that everything fell apart for Abe, Charles, and David. Their marriages expired with my parents, who had become a cohesive force for my brothers and their wives. Friday night dinners at Ralph and Luba's had succeeded in binding them all together, what with the homemade chicken soup, roast potatoes, brisket, Shabbos candles, and the one absent son and brother they shared. This should not have surprised me but it did. What's the opposite of cohesive? Enervating? Disintegrative? That had been my experience of my parents. That had been David's experience, too, and he resented me because I had managed to escape, which he would tell me when we finally met ten years later. At the time I resurfaced, he was not only angry with me, but he was furious at my parents and felt cheated by us all.

There are some other things I found out that day at Abe's that Auntie Sallah revealed to my brothers just after Dad's funeral. She told them that Rachmil was married to someone else before the war and had a child. The same was true for our mother. Neither of their first families survived.

What? My parents went to their graves without telling us? Something so huge? No hint had been dropped that any of us could discern. What else didn't they tell us? I thought of the sepia photo my mother kept on her dresser, a picture of the wide-eyed young man she said was her brother who had gone out one morning for a newspaper and never returned. Could this have been her first husband? I wondered, then doubted it because such an open display in the bedroom she shared with Rachmil was unlikely.

"What sex were our half-siblings?"

Abe thought Dad had a boy, Mom a girl, but he didn't know for sure. It was all a secret, these other lives that remained buried in the past, a secret that not only our parents but also our aunts and uncles had managed to keep from us.

"You know how Auntie Basha always hated Mom?"

"And she didn't like any of us boys either."

Basha, the wife of my father's brother, Srulec, never failed to exhibit a sour expression on her face whenever we were there. I assumed she was just a bitter, unhappy woman, and didn't question why.

"Well, Dad's first wife was Basha's sister. Two brothers had married two sisters."

My jaw hit the floor. I could scarcely believe it. The story of my family reeked of Greek tragedy. Weren't Menelaus and Agamemnon brothers who wed sisters Helen and Clytemnestra — and with disastrous results?

Abe continued, "Basha never forgave Mom for her sister's displacement. She blamed her for stealing Dad, but his first wife had already been killed by the time Rachmil and Luba got together."

The thought of my parents having lived such full, if traumatic, early lives and not having shared this devastating information with us, stunned me, angered me, then flooded me with great sadness. It made me weep at our first reunion, and it makes me weep as I write these words. I wonder what Josh and Dana thought of these four grown men, their father and uncles, who sat bawling at the dinner table.

The day ended with Charles and Harvey taking me to see their law offices. Charles and David started a law firm together

and called it Chaiton & Chaiton, specializing in insolvency
and bankruptcy. They bought a parcel of land on Sheppard
Avenue just west of Yonge Street and built a marble palace in
my parents' name. On our tour, they pointed out the building's
cornerstone with its dedication to Ralph and Luba Chaiton.
Inside, the offices were lushly decorated in art deco style, and
there was even a well-equipped gym. No doubt, our parents
would have rejoiced in the grandeur of their *naches*. But to me,
it felt like a marble mausoleum, a little over-the-top, and it did
nothing to assuage my sadness.

Not long afterwards, my brother David sent me an intensely personal letter on the fine-quality stationery of Chaiton &
Chaiton, Barristers and Solicitors. It opened a window for me
into the affect my disappearance had on the family. The letter's
rancour took my breath away:

> *I last saw and spoke with you on the day of my*
> *wedding in August 1973. I never realized how*
> *fateful that day would be, that it would mark*
> *the last communication of any kind I would re-*
> *ceive from a brother and friend who I dearly*
> *loved — that is, until now.*
>
> *During the years that intervened, as you can*
> *well imagine, we all spoke frequently about the*
> *sting of your repudiation of the family and of*
> *each of us since one could hardly fail to take*
> *the matter personally. We could understand*
> *that the polarization of your views and phil-*
> *osophies from those held by our parents drove*
> *you out of the house at a relatively tender age.*
> *You were not unique in this. Growing up in*

the Chaiton household was indeed a challenge. But geographical separation was not enough. You felt it necessary to your own survival to ex-communicate those of us whose only crime was the harbouring of a natural love and affection. We tried to understand for in this we had no choice. Your decision has been made and it was executed with finality.

The emptiness in my own life was and continues to be profound. In this I am sure I echo the feelings of my other brothers.... You should never think, even for a moment that your departure from the family and your repudiation of our parents did not irrevocably alter their universe. Do not even think that the imbalance created by your departure was ever re-stabilized in some other workable configuration. Nature abhors a vacuum and the vacuum you left was abhorrent to all.

✳ ✳ ✳

That night, I had a dream that seemed almost biblical. I was walking down a street, probably Palmerston Avenue. I saw a young Mary Newberry pushing a carriage with a baby. I didn't say anything as I passed her on the street. She asked, "What's the matter, don't you say hello?" So I said hello and continued to walk. I came up to a gnarly old tree, which I sensed had something to do with my parents. Its trunk was partially split open and I could see a small yellowy-green snake rollercoasting through it. There were different kinds of fruit hanging off the tree: cherries, peaches or apples, plums, and grapes. As I wondered how a single tree could bear four different kinds of fruit, a ball of fur came tumbling down from it, bounced on the ground, then unfurled into a racoon and sauntered happily and comically away. I figured the different fruits had to be grafted onto an old stock (the ancient, semi-rotten trunk) and sure enough, I noticed there were four thin twiggy branches, coming straight out of the trunk, one on top of another, each bearing a different fruit. And when I awoke, I wondered what it all meant.

I hadn't seen Mary in ages and were I to see her, I would definitely say hello. Also, in the dream, unlike in real life, she is young and has a baby. Why? Was she showing me a need to acknowledge the past, as it gives birth to the future? The gnarly old tree has a wound revealing a snake slithering through it, with its own undulating path and hidden life. But why does it have four fruits? Are these my brothers, each with his own precarious individuality, grafted onto the old stock of my parents, in an unnatural attachment: fruit hanging from thin, twiggy, straight branches that can easily snap off? Grapes, which don't even grow on trees — can that be David? The raccoon shows resilience from a fall, walking away from the tree unscathed in an idiosyncratic escape. I guess that's me: I walked away, but hardly unscathed.

* * *

I inquired about Dad's will. Charles had acted as Executor, and I asked him for a copy. Our father had left an estate that was valued at a million dollars and was to be divided equally among his five sons. I felt conflicting emotions. I was amazed at the size of my father's estate — a million dollars in 1985 on a tailor's income? I was proud of him and proud that I had never taken any large gifts from him. But everything seemed different now. Reluctantly, I asked Charles for my share. He hemmed and hawed and said that, since I could not be found when dad died, the other four had divided up my share among them. I was angry that Charles hadn't voluntarily mentioned this. I would have let this go except that our group at this point was destitute, and my father's will was his will: He had not disinherited me. We had sold our house in Toronto to finance our commitment to Rubin Carter's liberation, and all our money was gone. A little was coming in from our book, but that was it. My brothers refused to budge, and I was left with no choice but to initiate a lawsuit — Chaiton v Chaiton, so to speak. It soon became clear in court that Charles had no legal leg to stand on and he conceded as pretrial motions were underway. I received, along with the two hundred thousand dollars, not a little additional ill will from my brothers, a collective cold shoulder that would last about a decade.

Not unsurprisingly, it would be my role in the freeing of Rubin Carter that would again bring me back to my brothers, with the opening of the film *The Hurricane*. It was the last major Hollywood release of the twentieth century and I was a character in it, portrayed by Liev Schreiber. The Norman Jewison film, based in part on our book, starred Denzel Washington and was number one at the box office in Canada for three consecutive weeks. My brothers thought it a mind-blowing achievement, and reached out to me with congratulations. A reunion was imminent.

* * *

Terry Swinton (*right*), Rubin Carter, and me, at home in King City, Canada, 1992.

While Rubin was part of our family, we were able to have a significant impact on the state of criminal justice in Canada and in the United States. After *Lazarus and the Hurricane* was published, we were enlisted to join a committee seeking justice for Guy Paul Morin, who had been wrongly convicted of the murder of a nine-year-old girl. Rubin and I visited Paul in the Kingston Penitentiary, and Rubin's mere presence in the courtroom at Paul's bail hearing for release pending a likely successful appeal, sent a strong message to the judge that Morin was innocent. In February 1993, Paul was granted bail, and two years later was exonerated by DNA evidence that excluded him as the perpetrator. It wasn't until October 2020 when the girl's real killer, Calvin Hoover, a friend of the victim's parents, was finally named, having been pinpointed by genealogical evidence and confirmed through his own DNA.

Flush from our success in that case, Terry, Rubin, and I had a meeting with several lawyers (James Lockyer, Paul Copeland, and Peter Meier) at our house, where we founded the Association in Defence of the Wrongly Convicted, now Innocence Canada. Innocence Canada has been, and continues to be, instrumental in the exonerations of a surprising and growing number of innocent people, including David Milgaard and Steven Truscott and, more recently, seven individuals convicted of murdering a child in their care, based on the unreliable, flawed testimony of former doctor and pathologist Charles Smith. Shockingly, over one-third of wrongful convictions listed in the Canadian Registry of Wrongful Convictions, as author and law professor Kent Roach points out, are for "imagined crimes that never happened."[12]

In 1994, Rubin and I travelled to Northwestern University in Chicago, where law professor Larry Marshall, impressed by our success in Rubin's case, invited us to participate in a rally on behalf of Rolando Cruz, an innocent man on Illinois's death row. We visited with Bernardine Dohrn, whose office was next to Marshall's. I had met her previously at an American Bar Association conference in New Mexico, where Rubin was invited to speak. Bernardine was the former member of the Weather Underground who J. Edgar Hoover had called "the most dangerous woman in America." On the FBI's Top Ten Most Wanted List, she lived underground for more than a decade before resurfacing and being cleared of all alleged wrongdoing. She was now a law professor and leading advocate for the legal rights of children. At the bar association conference, I had given Bernardine a copy of *Lazarus and the Hurricane*, which she later passed on to Larry Marshall.

Rubin's presence and talk in Chicago was electrifying and galvanizing. Not only was Rolando Cruz eventually cleared and released from prison, but his exoneration led to an investigation by Northwestern journalism students into other death row cases, resulting in new evidence and the release of a dozen other innocent men awaiting execution. The sanctity of the state's capital convictions was called into question and the governor, George Ryan, issued a moratorium on the death penalty in Illinois, which was ultimately abolished in 2011.

In the early nineties, after one of his many forays back to the U.S., Rubin Carter returned to Toronto deathly ill. Too embarrassed to get in touch, he went to stay with our friend, Cree elder Vern Harper, who called to let us know of Rubin's condition. We felt completely responsible for him. We picked him up and took him straight to our family doctor, who hospitalized him immediately. A plethora of tests revealed he had TB, unknowingly contracted during an epidemic in Rahway State Prison in his last year there and lying dormant until he became run down. We brought him back into our house and nursed him slowly back to health. After months of taking medication, he started to feel better and went for a medical checkup. When told by his doctor that a blood test confirmed the infection was still active, he decided to leave. Nothing and no one could persuade him to stay. He felt fine, and thought what the doctor had said was just another trap. He scurried out of the house, leaving the rest of his medication behind, with dire consequences.

Late one evening a few months later, we accepted his collect call. Rubin was on his way back to Toronto for a talk and reading we had arranged as part of an International Literacy Day program ("How Literacy Helped Hurricane!") at the Palmerston Public Library. Rubin pulled over at a rest stop on the New York State Thruway; there was pain in his right eye that was so excruciating, he couldn't continue driving. I hopped on a plane to Rochester and took a hundred-dollar cab ride to the rest stop on the Thruway, where I found Rubin lying in the back of his Jeep pickup, moaning, his eyes covered. I gave him some 222s (Aspirin with codeine) to ease the pain, jumped into the driver's seat, and drove the four hours back to Toronto.

A doctor determined that the TB attacked Rubin's blind eye and attached itself to the stitches that were left from a prison operation years earlier. Although already blind in that eye, Rubin didn't want to lose it. Lisa and Paulene, who had joined the commune in 1981 and had trained in England as a nurse, spelled each other off, putting drops hourly in his eye all day and all night to try to save it. This went on for several days, to no avail. The eye had to be surgically removed.

In the hospital, under sedation before the surgery, Rubin was uncharacteristically talkative. He flashed back to when he was a youth in the Jamesburg Reformatory, where he got beaten up for wetting his bed.

"They made me hang my sheet out to dry on the clothesline so everyone could see."

The tough guy had disappeared. Shame was written on Rubin's face. It was soon overtaken by fear of being alone.

"Promise me you'll be here when I wake up."

The operation was long but successful. He had to get a glass eye. Again, we nursed him back to health before he disappeared. This was to be the last time. It was 1994, nine years after he walked out of prison. After that, there was no direct communication between us.

This seems shocking, but not in retrospect.

The day you leave prison is the day your sentence begins.

You don't spend twenty years behind bars — especially for something you didn't do, something you were accused of simply because of your race — and walk away unscathed. Nor do you have relationships that would in any way be considered normal, certainly not without extensive therapy. This statement applies to all sorts of cases of serious trauma. It applied to Rubin, who was incarcerated simply because he was Black; it applied to my parents who were imprisoned not because of anything they'd done, but simply because they were Jews.

In the 1990s, new laws were passed in the United States that effectively curtailed prisoner access to habeas corpus, which is the principle and mechanism, dating back to the Magna Carta and rooted in English Common Law, under which the legality of a prisoner's detention is subject to judicial scrutiny. Today, if Rubin Carter were applying for a writ of habeas corpus, as Judge Sarokin testified at a hearing on habeas corpus before the Congressional Judiciary Committee on Civil and Constitutional Rights, his petition would be pre-emptively denied. He had slipped through the eye of a needle and that eye is now shut, especially given twenty-first century anti-terrorism laws.

There is a coterie of pro-prosecution elements in New Jersey that still, more than a half century after the original events, continue to repeat the lies long since discredited, to

Rubin Carter and me in Las Vegas, where "Hurricane" was awarded the WBC Championship Belt, 1993.

spew their hatred of Rubin Carter wherever they can. Denzel Washington, who won the best actor Golden Globe for his portrayal of the Hurricane, was effectively denied an Oscar for his outstanding performance on account of a carefully or-chestrated telephone campaign to members of the Academy of Motion Picture Arts and Sciences that to award Denzel with an Oscar for portraying Carter would be to heap praise on a triple murderer. Even today, after an inspiring online article entitled "Worldwide Hurricane" by Nobel Peace Prize nominee David Swanson was republished on Scoop News, it received a vitriolic letter from someone claiming to be part of an organization called "Friends of the Victims of Rubin Carter." Rubin Carter's last act before he died on Easter Sunday 2014 was to advocate on behalf of Brooklyn's David McCallum. But it made no difference to them. McCallum would prove to be yet another link in a seemingly endless chain of wrongful convictions. He was exonerated and released just months after Rubin's death. I can hear Rubin's spirit chuckling in the afterlife, "Motherfuckers!"

15

The First Law of Thermodynamics

IN THE MILLENNIAL YEAR, ABE HAD A NEW BABY daughter and invited me to a party at his house to welcome her into the world. He named her Luba after our mother and in her honour. David was there, and it was the first time I'd seen him since his wedding some thirty years earlier. It was also the first time in three decades that all five brothers were together.

My relationship with my brothers had always been very physical. Whenever we found ourselves in the same room, we would draw even closer together as if by some animal magnetism, a litter of puppies jostling over one another, a paw in the face, a push to the floor, a rollover, a yap, a knee to the gut, a capitulation, an unthinking embrace, arms draped over shoulders like floppy ears, a howl, a growl, a nudge. This canine chaos

The five Chaiton brothers together for the first time in twenty-seven years, 2000. *From the left*: Harvey, Abe, me, Charles, and David.

was the tenor of our childhood lives. We were so much older now, but our arms still draped around one another and I felt a connection from our youth resurging. We had a group picture taken, the Chaiton boys. It was as if we'd been prisoners of war together and this was our reunion. And I felt a deep sadness, as did Abe, that our parents were not there to enjoy their new granddaughter, who could not replace our mother, but would grow up to be another remarkable woman named Luba.

※ ※ ※

April 2003 well deserved its cruelest month appellation. We were in the midst of the SARS breakout. Lisa, who laughed at my self-absorption as a dancer, at my obsessive focus on my physical body, had not taken care of hers. She had a persistent cough for months, thinking it just a cold hanging on. I remember the day it was finally diagnosed. We were sitting in a small examination room at Princess Margaret Hospital. Everyone in the hospital had sanitized their hands and were wearing face masks, including Lisa, Paulene, and me. We waited in this claustrophobic space for what seemed like an eternity. Finally, a doctor entered. She spoke hesitatingly. I couldn't see her lips moving behind her mask. The sound was muffled, and this is what I heard: "Esophageal cancer … inoperable … three months to live … chemotherapy might give you an extra month…. Sorry."

The doctor quickly disappeared, leaving us alone. The news was so bad we didn't believe it. It was inconsistent with our invincibility. I questioned whether the face mask had altered the words and maybe we hadn't heard correctly. It started to sink in when we got home and had to break the news to everyone.

As a group, we inhaled, gathered our strength together, and focused on getting Lisa healed with the same determination had we put into freeing Rubin Carter. Lisa refused the chemotherapy so we had to go alternative, which is how we lived anyway. Terry, who had fiendishly researched obscure legal case precedents, now did the same with medical information. Lisa's diet was radically changed to organic vegetarian, lots of freshly made fruit and vegetable juices. She went to see a naturopath, got high dosages of vitamin C intravenously, and took other supplements, including reishi and cordyceps mushrooms, which were recommended by our dear family doctor, Kenneth Chen.

We enlisted the help of our Cree family, elder Pauline Shirt and her son Clayton, who had lived with us in King Township for a year when Rubin was still part of our household. Clayton was severely dyslexic, and his early Eurocentric schooling in the public system was inadequate and didn't speak to him as a First Nations youth. Even the Wandering Spirit School that his mom and dad, Vern Harper, founded specifically to foster education based on Indigenous perspectives, culture, and history, had left his level of literacy wanting. I taught Clayton to read at age nineteen, not an easy task for him but one that showed his determination and strength of character. When he was with us, he grew out his hair and transformed himself from a rebellious teenager who was into the grunge scene and rejected Indigeneity into a firekeeper. Today he has tenure as the Traditional Knowledge Keepers' Elder at the Indigenous Resource Centre of the University of Toronto.

Clayton invited his teacher, Vicky "One Side Moccasin," a Lakota medicine woman, to his sister's place at Rama Reserve, where they held a sweat lodge ceremony for Lisa. Everyone in our house attended, including Natacha, Axelle, and Sharangabo, three survivors of the Rwandan genocide. All of us humbly presented tobacco and entered the lodge on our knees, then sat cross-legged in the dark in a tight circle with members of Clayton's family. Vicky welcomed us and spoke of the suffering she was feeling in the lodge from our African brothers and sisters, who had made the journey across the big water to Turtle Island. As steam rose from the rocks at the circle's centre, we all felt connected, united by the intensifying heat, mutually supportive, caring for and carrying one another, our energies focused on light and healing. We had another ceremony with Vicky a week later at a lodge near Sault Ste. Marie.

With all this love, we were certain Lisa was going to survive. The doctors prescribed liquid morphine for her, but she was able to get by with just extra strength Tylenols, and that was a good sign. But we were deluding ourselves. Lisa became uncharacteristically depressed. She seemed stuck, at times, in her childhood, in a miserable place from where ghosts and past fears resurfaced. She was scared and vulnerable, her nerves ajar, her natural optimism in eclipse. She reviewed her life, questioned the wisdom of everything she'd done, veering uneasily between distress and clarity.

October arrived and, with it, another perspective. I attended a screening of the documentary *The Weather Underground* at the Bloor Cinema in Toronto, where I again had an opportunity to speak with Bernardine Dohrn. She greeted me warmly and said, "You got the ball rolling. You were the guys that started it all!"

I was bowled over, especially as the remark came from a true American revolutionary I so deeply admired, an antiwar activist whose profound understanding of the unfair advantages of white privilege grounded her lifelong commitment to interracial justice and equity. I couldn't wait to convey her sentiments to Lisa, who, less than a week from death, was deeply questioning the value of her life.

"Really? Bernardine said that?"

That she did so gave Lisa much comfort.

Living in Kleinburg, we went for walks in the woods on the grounds of the McMichael Gallery. We watched and relished the industry of beavers in the Humber River, wreaking havoc with the saplings on the banks as they built their massive structures. As Lisa's strength was waning, we strolled arm in arm around our garden, sat for hours, silent and blissful, in the early autumn sun. While she was getting the vitamin C treatments, I read to her from Krishnamurti. I hadn't felt this close to her since before the Hurricane.

Only near the very end did she need the morphine. She lay all day on the couch in the living room, unable to move. When she couldn't be bothered to get up to go to the bathroom, I yelled at her, and was ashamed. I was angry that she was about to abandon me, us. She was barely present, could feel the draw of spirits. She said there were men she did not recognize who had come to visit her. She said they were telling her to just lie still for four days, and all would be fine.

Hallowe'en, just two days before Lisa's fifty-ninth birthday, was unusually hot. We were supposed to be going to a party that evening at the house of a close friend, Joanne McLean, the outstanding lawyer whose work with James Lockyer helped to free Guy Paul Morin. We hadn't had a play date with Joanne in ages. But this one was not to be.

Lisa sensed that the end was near. I had a premonition, too. The night before her last day on earth, I dreamed that she had climbed onto Lakota, the wilder and more spirited of our horses, and despite our warnings that she didn't know how to ride, Lisa galloped off into the distance.

We all knew it was the end when Lisa begged us for just one more day. It was a wish we could not fulfill. She assured us that we were going to be okay when she was gone. Terry, Paulene, Kathy, and I were with her when she took her last breath and left.

And we cried.

I've never shed so many tears. In fact, I cried for seven days, while friends came and went, bringing us food. Pauline Shirt and her sons, Clayton and Les, and her son-in-law, Derek, held a ceremony in Lisa's room, smudging it with smoking cedar greens, then drumming and chanting prayers around her empty bed. Derek had made the drum he was playing and presented it to us as a gift. We kept a fire going in our fireplace for the full week.

That Lisa of all people — indomitable, vital, fiercely energetic, committed to life, and repulsed by death — could die made no sense, and violated the laws of nature and principles of the universe. "Energy can neither be created nor destroyed." Wasn't that the universal law? Yet death seemed to be an energy destroyer. Without Lisa's hearty laugh, the sound of the world seemed depleted; without her fulsome presence, the world felt emptier, one great soul less, a muchness less.

Lisa's body was in a funeral home, awaiting cremation. Terry and I couldn't face going. Our Cree family helped prepare her body for the journey into the next world by placing wooden match sticks in between her fingers to help light her way and a medicine bag around her neck for protection. Kathy and Paulene went to see her, and they said she looked young and beautiful. Pauline Shirt thought so, too.

Lisa visited me in my dreams every night. The fourth night I was lying prone on my bed, trying to fall asleep. Suddenly, I felt a weight on my body, as if someone were lying on top of me, embracing me from behind. I was sure it was Lisa, hugging me, saying her final goodbye. I knew I had to let her go.

We had a memorial for her at our Kleinburg home and close to a hundred people came to celebrate her life. We huddled in the living room, a fire roaring. People spoke to the group as the feeling arose, telling loving stories of the profound impact Lisa had on their lives. Poet, author, and historian Afua Cooper, present with daughters Lami and Habiba, wrote a fierce dub poem for her, which we distributed to everyone on scrolls as a memento. Auntie Bea, Paulene's aunt who loved Lisa, sang a hymn a cappella. Guy Paul Morin came to represent his family, his sisters, mother Ida, and father Alphonse with whom we had been very close. Joanne McLean, of course, was there. Present, too, was Maestro Fresh Wes whom over the years Lisa had inspired with great old music from our vinyl collection; and broadcaster/journalist Norman "Otis" Richmond commented on what an attentive listener Lisa had been. Louis Alexakos, an old-world hat tailor we worked with, and his wife, Poppy, came laden with trays of Greek food she had baked. Many Rwandans attended, some even driving from Montreal and Ottawa. Mama Janine arrived with a silver-framed poem that she had written for Lisa, which she recited. Arthur Lockhart, a criminal justice professor at Humber College and dear friend, came to pay his respects. As did Higinia Natoli and daughters Kira and Marla, and actor/storyteller Sandra Whiting. I invited Abe and he arrived with Luba, who played with the other children present. Abe didn't know Lisa but had an idea of how much she had meant to me. It was the first time any blood relative had been in my home, and I was touched.

To remember and honour Lisa, every month on the night of the full moon, I would take that drum out of its cloth bag and strike it, while thinking of her. This ritual was to continue for seven years, and it was just between us — I never told anyone about it.

* * *

Another way of dealing with grief is to transmute earth-shattering loss into something vibrant and alive, something with longevity, if not immortality. For me, that meant creating a work of art, a compulsion so strong in me that I couldn't ignore it. Indeed, it felt like it was the only way I was going to be able to survive.

Our household at this time, as I mentioned, was graced by the presence of Rwandans. Che Rupari — a Tutsi who had grown up in Burundi and moved to Ottawa in the early eighties at age eleven with his mother, brother, and sister — was the first to come live with us. Lisa and I were introduced to him at a coffee shop by Mimi, a young Rwandan woman we had hired at Big It Up, a fashion hat retail and wholesale business we began in 1996 with Paulene's cousin Dameion, a Jamaican Canadian in his early twenties, whose creativity and dynamism we loved and who was now living with us.

We hit it off instantly with Che, who was tall, gregarious, with a wonderful sense of humour. He'd never been with white people before who shared food with him so freely. ("I couldn't believe it," he'd later reveal. "Biting from the same cookie!") It didn't take long before he was working at Big It Up, then also moving in. Che then introduced us to Sharangabo, who had survived the Rwandan genocide and recently arrived in Canada. Tall and good-looking, with smooth, dark skin, he had an amazing smile and an easygoing charm and laugh that belied his past trauma. From time to time, he would drop by our Big It Up office, and we'd sit on the couch in our kitchen area and talk. He, like Che, felt comfortable with us and gradually opened up about his experiences in the genocide five years earlier, when he was fourteen years old.

It was gut-wrenching. So little was known in the West at this time about what had happened in Rwanda in 1994, when close to a million people, primarily Tutsis, were slaughtered. As Sharangabo spoke about his personal experiences, I couldn't help thinking that they were similar to what my parents must have gone through in the Holocaust, even though I did not know this as a fact. There was something hauntingly familiar about what Sharangabo told us, maybe not the specifics but the emotional landscape of genocide. He seemed relieved to be sharing the burden of his experience. And I thought, everyone knows about the Holocaust but nobody knows about this, a Holocaust that happened in our own lifetime — and that someone so young is a survivor, here in the flesh, testifying!

Sharangabo had a scar at the back of his neck and another going down his arm, where he'd been chopped by a machete. Presumed dead, he was thrown onto a truck for disposal. This was after he witnessed the slaughter of his uncle. His father had been murdered, too. I asked if he would mind if I made notes as we talked, not knowing exactly what I wanted them for. I just knew there was a story here that cried out to be told.

Our household soon became younger, more Black than white, more Rwandan than Jamaican. Natacha, originally from Burundi as was Che, escaped Rwanda with her family by going through the Hôtel des Milles Collines (Hotel Rwanda), where her father, a prominent judge, had to pay a significant amount of money for their brief stay before they were able to board a U.N. plane and flee. Axelle's experience was more traumatic. One of her classmates, a notorious Hutu genocidaire, was on the prowl, hunting specifically for her; for weeks during the genocide, she hid in a hole in the ground, starving and terrified.

When Natacha and Axelle came to Canada in 2001, their arrival was delayed one week because of the 9/11 grounding of planes. They moved into our Kleinburg house not long after, and began to help out at Big It Up, while we sorted out their immigration and education, which had been interrupted by the genocide. Axelle aced a first-year university course and qualified for and was accepted into York University. We helped Natacha get into the Transitional Year Programme at the University of

Toronto, where she excelled and was honoured as class valedictorian. Sharangabo, with our support, would also go through the program and earn a bachelor's degree. There was a period when I held weekly English grammar, essay writing, and literature classes at Big It Up for this amazing group of eager and engaged students: Dameion and Che, who were taking philosophy courses at York University; Sharangabo, Natacha, and Axelle. Natacha, who would study Ojibway at the University of Toronto, was interested in First Nations history and culture, and her presence at the sweat lodges for Lisa was a firsthand experience her classmates could only dream of. Axelle and Natacha both now have doctorates and teach at prominent universities in the States, Natacha at the University of Chicago and Axelle at Penn State. Sharangabo and Che now live and work back home in Rwanda.

Soon after Lisa died, I sat down to write. It was going to be a screenplay for a movie to let the world know what had happened in Rwanda in 1994 and its parallels to the Holocaust fifty years earlier. No movies were widely released and few books were written about the Rwandan genocide at that time. I didn't know it then, but learning about Rwanda was going to lead me to learn about the Holocaust. And the screenplay I was writing, which was to morph into a stage play, was going to help me get in touch with my family's story as well.

I created two main characters, both survivors, one inspired by Sharangabo and the other a Jewish tailor like my father. I didn't know how these two would meet, until one day, while watching the local CBC news, I caught an interview with Paula David. She was a senior social worker at the Baycrest Geriatric Centre, with over a hundred Holocaust survivors in its care. Paula spoke about the Holocaust Survivor Program and the sensitivity training she had begun for the staff at Baycrest. She talked about short-term memories becoming impaired as we age and long-term memories coming to the fore, and how our childhood experiences become more vivid, while recent ones fade. For Holocaust survivors, Paula explained, that means childhood traumas resurface to traumatize again. Her program trained caregivers, hospital staff, and personal support workers to be sensitive to that reality, to understand and try to avoid possible triggers, like going to the showers or seeing doctors in white lab coats for medical testing.

It was an *aha!* moment for me, and I arranged to meet Paula at her office at Baycrest to find out more. She was immediately enthusiastic and generous in sharing information. We have since become good friends.

The idea for the play was to have the young Rwandan survivor working as a personal support worker at a place like Baycrest, where he comes into contact with the Jewish tailor, each of them knocking heads, locked into themselves, and totally ignorant of the other's experience. They go on to discover that the other is a genocide survivor, both then realizing the identicalness of their suffering and its origins in racial and ethnic hatred. For the old Jewish man, the deep bond they forge is closer than his familial relationships, specifically his relationship with his son.

I developed this story over many years. It was fictional but with a basis in truth. The Rwandan character was called Lion, after Sharangabo's other name, Ntare, which means "lioness" in Kinyarwanda. I changed his story to include an amalgam of details that I had heard and read from other survivors. I named the Jewish tailor Noah Goldblum. Not knowing my father's story, I invented a history for Noah that I thought was plausible. Noah, like my father, was convinced of the uniqueness of his suffering, which gave him licence to behave badly, resorting to humour and sarcasm as a mode of self-protection. He was someone with the ability to speak openly with strangers but not with his own offspring; someone who could put on a game face despite feeling weak, powerless, overwhelmed; someone who placed the highest value on his absolute aloneness; someone who was certain in the knowledge that nothing will ever be good, which provided him an odd sense of relief and freedom in never having to be disappointed.[13]

After a workshop, and later a staged reading at the Harbourfront Studio Theatre, we decided to put on a showcase production with sets and costumes by Teresa Przybylski, and a performing cast of eight. This would require a lot of fundraising. With Alon's assistance, I applied for and received a playwright's grant from the Toronto Arts Council, as well as substantial grants from the Ontario Arts Council and the Canada Council. Needing more funding for a large production, we put together a fundraising committee. Janet Rosenberg, the noted landscape architect and my brother Abe's then girlfriend, connected Alon and me to Barry Green, and we had a meeting with Barry and his brother David at Greenrock, their property management company corporate office. Not only were they taken by the project and would make a generous donation, Barry suggested we hold a fundraising reception at the top of the Sutton Place Hotel and that his youngest sister, Lindy, might be interested in joining the committee.

We had a committee meeting one morning in the small boardroom at Greenrock. We were just settling in around the round table, when this woman walked in, dressed in bell-bottom jeans, and took a seat at the table. She crossed her right leg over her left knee and, a needle and thread in hand, began to stitch up the unravelling hem on her jeans. I heard her say in a deep, rich voice that she's off for the weekend to see some art shows in Montreal. She seemed very self-possessed, intent on doing what she was doing, regardless of the eyes of strangers in the room. Her hair was in a straight, short bob with bangs, and dark except for a funky burgundy streak. And she was tall and beautiful. Who is this cool chick, I wondered, until I figured out this must be Lindy Green, Barry and David's sister.

The Sutton Place reception fundraiser, engagingly hosted by broadcaster Ralph Benmergui, was extraordinarily successful. In the anteroom, a United Nations Human Rights division and Aegis Trust exhibit of large-scale photographs entitled *Lessons from Rwanda* set the tone. Irwin Cotler, the former Minister of Justice and Attorney General, flew in from Ottawa to give the keynote address. Dr. James Orbinski, who had received the Nobel Peace Prize on behalf of Doctors Without Borders, was also to appear but, at the last minute, was unable to attend. Barry Green and director Alon Nashman also spoke.

In addition to members of the Green and Chaiton families, there were many notables in the audience, including Canadian TV personality Jeanne Beker, whose parents were Holocaust survivors; Leora Schaefer, the Director of Facing History and Ourselves Canada; and Holocaust survivor Joe Gottdenker. The response to the speeches, to a scene from the play with Paul Soles and Mighty Popo, and to music from the play performed by Popo, David Buchbinder, and Waleed Abdulhamid, with a song performed by Abena Malika, resulted in our raising close to a hundred thousand dollars.

The Showcase Production of *Noah's Great Rainbow* opened on March 28, 2009, at the Al Green Theatre in Toronto. It was

Jacques "Mighty Popo" Murigande (*left*) and Don Francks in my play, *Noah's Great Rainbow*, Al Green Theatre, Toronto, 2009.

preceded by a performance for Holocaust survivors at Baycrest and for a number of survivors from a growing Rwandan community in Toronto. I was apprehensive, but the performances were powerful and the play went over well, with many of the survivors from both communities, including my Auntie Sallah, fraternizing easily in the auditorium afterwards, their deep connection manifest. There were also several student performances during the run, with classes being bussed in from as far as Barrie, particularly those studying the new course on genocide being offered in grade eleven history. The play was a hit in many respects, having a powerful impact on the students especially and garnering generous feedback and audience comments.

The writing and work on the play felt like a step toward my father, engendering a feeling, if not an understanding, of what it was like to live in the mind of a survivor. Moreover, it opened my mind to the possibility of forgiveness. Perhaps the best thing about *Noah's Great Rainbow* was that it brought me and Lindy together. We've been partners ever since. And she was to seren-dipitously open the door that would finally reveal my parents' lives to me, and to my brothers, bringing us all closer together.

* * *

My brother Charles died of cancer in May 2010, and the five brothers were now four. It wasn't until the last few years of his life that I really got to know him. Contrary to the aloof, vola-tile, and unpredictable person that I thought he was when we were young, he had grown into a man who was warm, funny, unfailingly polite, considerate, and extremely generous. I spent a fair amount of time with Charles and his wife, Karen, during their struggle with seemingly endless treatments, recoveries, and relapses, and that's when Charles's true colours were re-vealed. He never failed to smile and crack jokes. Informed he had brain cancer, he was asked if he'd agree to an operation.

"Well, that's a no-brainer, Doctor," he answered.

I still marvel at his quiet strength and determination. Never once did I hear him curse his lot or say, "Why me?" For Charles, it was always, "Why shouldn't it be me? Should it be someone else instead?" And yet I knew his suffering was tremendous.

I visited Charles with greater frequency the closer he came to death. When he was completely bedridden and could no longer see, I sat at his bedside and read out loud to him. I remember a few days before he died, reading from Bernice Eisenstein's memoir *I Was a Child of Holocaust Survivors* about the author's experiences growing up in Toronto, her parents concentration camp survivors, her life uncannily similar to ours. Bernice's memories of Kensington Market, poker playing, Bar Mitzvahs, and her use of Yiddish phrases stirred Charles, who at this time could scarcely move or barely stay awake. Yet, as I read, his body seemed to come alive, his mind racing back in time, his hand clenching mine in sheer bliss. We were never closer.

I am sorry that Charlie missed the astounding revelations ahead, beginning just a month after he died. That's when Lindy's exhibition of Maciej Frankiewicz's paintings took place and I found out that my father's words had been quoted in a leading Holocaust historian's new book.

16

Wierzbnik

FROM MY PERSPECTIVE, CHRISTOPHER R. Browning's groundbreaking work, *Remembering Survival: Inside a Nazi Slave-Labor Camp*, could have been called *What the Tailor Saw*. The moment the book is in my hands, I flip to the index. Chaiton, Rachmil. I gasp, spellbound. I can't believe what I'm reading. Chaiton, Israel (Uncle Srulec) is also referenced. And both are cited in footnotes throughout the book — Israel six times, my father, eleven — which also includes references to my father's other brother spelled here as Jankiel. Numerous other names resonate from my childhood, among them Howard Chandler, Michulek Baranek, Max Naiman, Beniek Zukerman, Manya Kaufman — and Mina Binsztok! Hidden family histoy is about to be disclosed in a hardcover book published by W.W. Norton & Company in 2010, twenty-five years after the death of my parents.

In his introduction, Browning writes about the Hamburg court trial of Walther Becker "for his role in the liquidation of the Jewish ghetto in Wierzbnik on October 27, 1942 — an action in which close to 4000 Jews were sent to their deaths in the gas chambers of Treblinka, some sixty to eighty Jews were murdered on the spot, and about 1,600 Jews were sent to three slave-labor camps in nearby Starachowice."[14]

Becker, the defendant, was in charge of the Nazi Security Police in the Radom district of Poland and was headquartered in Starachowice, ninety-five miles south of Warsaw. He claimed that after learning of the impending deportation, a decision that came down from on high, he observed the Roundup and the loading of Jews on the train, but neither participated nor gave any orders.

In 1972, the trial court issued its judgment. The judge disbelieved all the Jewish witnesses, which included my father, because they were not "indifferent, attentive, intelligent observer[s]." He ruled that eyewitness testimony, especially by witnesses who were not "disinterested" and "distanced" was "the most unreliable form of evidence" and should be disregarded as a matter of principle.[15] He concluded that Becker's account was not contradicted by any credible evidence, and Becker was acquitted. For Browning, the judge's verdict was "an egregious miscarriage of justice."[16] *Remembering Survival* was born out of a desire to balance the scales and to give Becker, at the very least, "his appropriate place in historians' hell."[17] Browning's project soon broadened into the first comprehensive look into the little-known phenomenon of the factory slave-labour camp, using Starachowice as a case study.

Once I get a sense of the trial and of the man my father testified against, I skip to the Chaiton-referenced pages. I learn that my father, as a tailor, had the putative good fortune to work inside Becker's police headquarters and "occasionally had to visit Becker's office to make clothing for the Germans."[18] He later provided, in deposition and testimony, what Browning described as a "harrowing account"[19] of what went on there. Becker was the one who gave the orders, but the infliction of torture was left to others. Indeed, when Uncle Srulec was arrested for picking up a lump of coal along a railway track, "Becker screamed that he should confess to sabotage, and someone else beat him."[20]

My skimming is halted at a single paragraph concerning and quoting my father, about the liquidation of the Jewish ghetto, the central issue of Becker's trial. This is not a movie, not a scene from *Schindler's List*, I tell myself. These are my father's words memorialized in black and white between the hardcovers of an important book. I have trouble focusing. I reread the words many times over before my mind begins to unfreeze, allowing their import to sink in:

> The tailor Rachmil Chaiton had already been promised that the skilled craftsmen like himself would remain with their entire families — in this case, a wife and child. Thus, when the call for those with work cards went out, he approached Becker on the marketplace for permission to take his wife and child with him. Becker said he could take his wife but not "the little shit" ("*die kleine Scheisse*"), indicating the child. "We naturally did not want to separate from our child. I was forced to join the row of Jews

chosen for work, while my wife remained
with the child and … was deported."[21]

My father is not testifying — he is talking to me at last! He
is telling me about his first wife and child and what became of
them. Tailoring saved his life and could have saved his wife, but
not the child. He was admitting to being a father who could
not protect his child. And he ended up not saving his wife
either because she stayed with their child. His wife, my Auntie
Basha's sister, selflessly went to certain death so her child would
not suffer alone. No wonder my aunt hated my mother for re-
placing her saintly sister, a martyr who, it turns out, perished in
Treblinka. Did my father regret not remaining with his child,
as his wife had done? He says he didn't want to separate from
them but was forced to join those chosen for work. Or did he
feel that his work card as a tailor was worth too much to gain-
say its benefits? Did fear get the better of him? Surely, he had to
have been drowning in survivor guilt — and this, even before
the war had ended.

So there it is. Rachmil had a previous family and this is now
confirmed as gospel truth by my father himself. Jesus. Wait till
I tell my brothers. We really did have a half-sibling … even if
it was "a little shit." I google the word "*Scheisse*" to see if it will
give some clue as to the sex of the child. *Die Scheisse* is femin-
ine, but that doesn't mean the child was necessarily a girl. Even
a little boy would be called *Die Scheisse*.

Shit!

I have to find out more. If this wealth of information is
in the book, what else is in the original transcripts? I need to
get hold of them, but how? Get in touch with the German
Consulate? Fear rises in my throat, and I feel queasy. Why

not ask Christopher Browning directly? He'll know. A quick read of the jacket cover points me to the history department at the University of North Carolina. Browning's email address is listed on its website. I write, explaining who I am, what I am searching for. Not ten minutes pass before my email is answered. He has the transcripts! He will be in Toronto in a few weeks for a speaking engagement at Beth Tzedec synagogue, part of Holocaust Education Week, and he can give them to me then or he can send them now. And he tells me they're in German.

Please send them, I reply.

* * *

The bomb comes in the mail. Not email, because letter bombs don't usually arrive that way, but via snail mail that inches into my home one fine fall day, one of those rare days taken off from work at Big It Up with a thought, however humbly repressed, of celebrating what is generally considered a landmark birthday. Six zero, round and full, five even dozens, has gravitas on the metric and imperial scales, is perhaps the culmination of half a biblical man's life, and the beginning of a second half that will never be completed — a half life, as it were. Turning sixty is some big deal. And for me, the day I turned sixty, the world's axis wobbled.

My mind, I've discovered, has been coloured by a certainty that nothing is really knowable. It's a lesson my survivor parents unwittingly imparted to me. "*Freg nisht!*" the retort to "So ask me how I am?" is more than a Yiddish punchline. Asking a personal question is fraught with the likelihood of stumbling on horrors that could again be loosed upon the world.

A question could ignite a fuse, explode with sudden ferocity, wreak untold anguish. An answer could lay waste cities. So don't ask. Don't ask. *Freg nisht.*

Under this imperative, all is choked, stifled, hidden. Subtext is felt but impossible to decipher. The story of my family history, of my parents' lives, forever out of reach, ungraspable in the formless haze. With no freedom to explore, curiosity loses its drive, dissipates, falls dormant. Lack of clarity becomes a chronic condition whose outward symptoms are a blank politeness and lack of affect.

How often have I found myself beset by feelings buried but present in the way a pervasive, persistent odour is present — its source indeterminate, its ability to assail the olfactory sense remaining just below consciousness, prompting an occasional reflexive sniff followed by a shrug and the resumption of the task at hand? Sensory doubt engenders a kind of existential vagueness, or is it vice versa? I constantly second-guess myself: Did I really hear what I heard? See what I saw? Feel what I felt? and invariably come up with "Nah."

It's now in my hands, this manila envelope the postal worker has just delivered. How ironic that it should come today. I examine it carefully. It is addressed to me in hasty handwritten black ink from Chapel Hill, Professor Christopher R. Browning, University of North Carolina, $2.07 U.S. postage. I wonder about the cost of opening it.

I carry it like a paper phylactery up the stairs to my bedroom and set it down beside a Collins German Dictionary on my desk. I hesitate, wanting to know and not wanting to know, wanting to know and wanting not to know. My parents had their reasons for wanting us not to know — their emotional and psychic survival depended on it, and my survival, I realize, depends on its opposite. Details. Specifics. Light. Despite the intense conditioning of my youth and the long passage of years, my desire for information still burns, has not been completely extinguished. The "don't ask" dictate be damned. There are doors, and envelopes, that must be opened. That I'm finally going to open. That I am opening. Finally.

I slide the serrated edge of a knife across the top of the envelope. Reaching in, I draw out what looks like censored prison correspondence with names of people and places redacted in thick black marker.

The first document is my father's sworn deposition taken at the Consulate General of the Federal Republic of Germany in Toronto on September 28, 1966. It was originally in English but translated in German for the benefit of the Hamburg court. Rachmil tells me he was born in Kovel, but his mother had been born in Starachowice, the town to where the entire family moved in 1930 and where he was working as a tailor when the war broke out. After the occupation, the Gestapo needed a good tailor, and Rachmil was recommended by the *Judenrat* (Jewish council). He thus became the Gestapo's tailor and was provided with an assistant. He goes on to talk about the Roundup and Becker's role in it:

> In the deportation operation, Becker shot many people. He ran crazily around on this day with a pistol in his hand. I saw him and asked him what would happen to me and my family. He said, "You can stay, your wife too, but" — pointing to the child — "throw the little shit away." Since my wife would not let go of the child, a Lithuanian from the guard

force struck her on her head with a stick and dragged her away with the child. I was prevented from following my wife. Becker saw and tolerated everything. I never saw my wife and child again.[22]

There follows a litany of additional horrors Rachmil describes:

After the inventory, when the deportees and the craftsmen had already been separated, an old, bent-over man was walking across the Market Square. Becker went to him and shot him in the neck. I saw it myself; it was on the corner, where Niskas Street enters Market Square.... I saw the following in Fall 1942: About 10 Poles had been caught in the forest and were brought to the camp. There, 2 Jews, one of them my uncle Nussen Winograd, had to dig graves. Before the work was complete, Becker, who was standing there, gave the command to shoot the 2 Jews; the order was then followed. I saw this from the Konsumbaracke. Subsequently, the 10 Poles were also shot.... In winter 1942,... numerous security officers ... as well as Becker came into the camp. I had exited my barracks and lay on the grass so I could see what was going on. The people went to the hospital barracks that was perched above us since the camp was on the edge of a slope. The sick people were driven out of the barracks and shot as they walked down the stairs to the lower part of the camp. The next day, I went over to the bodies and found a young man still alive. He had only been shot through the ear. I hid him in my barracks and had him treated by a doctor who was also a prisoner (D. Kramass, died in Auschwitz). Later I could accommodate the wounded man at work at SS-man Frania's. Frania was good to us and was punished as a result and imprisoned. The young Jew is still alive, as far as I know, in the USA, but I unfortunately forgot his name.

In the Dugaj forest, about 120 prisoners were shot one day in spring 1943. They had been brought there by truck. While I was in the steam bath, SS-man Mayer entered wearing a uniform that was splattered with blood, and I asked him where the blood came from. He said that he brought several people to another camp and had a nosebleed on the way. A few days later, I spoke to some Poles who told me that there was a large gravesite in the Dugaj forest that still moves and where hands and feet stick out of the earth.[23]

He speaks of witnessing other murders, then continues: "Often, when Becker or others came to try on clothes, I heard them boast of their shootings while they waited. They would ask questions, such as: How many have you shot? I bumped off three. I can no longer remember precisely who said what.

About Becker, I still remember that he had a long scar on his neck up to his chin. He had gray hair and was around 50 at the time."[24]

I continue reading, struggling with the German, devastated by its content, but needing finally to know. I manage to maintain my composure until I start learning about my mother: "Althoff [a director of the slave camp Luba worked in] was an ethnic German, previously had another name, and whose mother was Jewish — my current wife met her in Auschwitz and spoke to her, during which she told her that her son was an SA-man — wore an SA uniform with a swastika."[25]

This is the first time I have heard that my mother was in Auschwitz! Until this moment, I believed that both she and my dad had only been in Bergen-Belsen. "I saw Schroth [commander of the Ukrainian guards] another time as he was urinating into a grave in which 12 Jews who had died of typhus lay. Among them was the husband of my current wife. While he urinated, he said something to the effect of 'here lies the shit.'" Rachmil says he can name other witnesses to these events. The first he mentions is "My wife, Mrs. Luba Chaiton, first married name Rotvoegel, maiden name Kirschenblum, who was also in the Majowska camp and whose child from her first marriage was killed in her presence."[26]

An unearthly sound arises from so deep within me that my entire body is convulsed by uncontrollable howls of such eerie intensity that my housemates Terry, Kathy, Paulene, Dameion, and Che come running from the floor below to see what's wrong. The most I can utter is "My parents ..." My body continues to be racked by this blinding insight into their history and their suffering. I can't stop sobbing. I'm rattled by the abrupt termination of my sixty years of ignorance, and I am overwhelmed by guilt, shattered by my failure to have given them sufficient berth with which to have manoeuvred their fraught new country lives. Will I ever be forgiven?

Held and comforted by my friends, I feel no comfort. Terry urges me to desist from reading further but I'm too far down this road to turn back. From the transcript, I find out that Rachmil was shipped to Auschwitz as well. It was Becker, my father testified, who directed "the loading to Auschwitz. He stood by the train. The train cars were packed too fully; I was lucky and was in an open train car, so I had air. Many people died in the enclosed cars."[27] That both my parents were prisoners in Auschwitz I could easily have determined from their number tattoos had I done even a cursory search online; but I hadn't. Why not? Out of deference to their silence or to my not being ready, prior to this, to deal with what I may have found?

My persistence is rewarded with a key fact my father tells me in his subsequent 1970 testimony, the second document in Browning's package, about the marketplace Selection: "We received an order to walk to the Market Square. My wife, my then two-and-half-year-old boy and I made our way ..."[28]

The shit was a boy! Tell me again what happened, *Tateh*:

> We took hand baggage with us that we had already packed. I had already heard ... that a deportation was imminent and that we craftsmen along with our entire families would continue to be employed in a factory....
>
> En route to Market Square, we already started hearing shots and saw dead bodies by the side of the road. There was also a substantial number of dead bodies at the Market

Square when we arrived ... My wife and I
wanted to take our child with us to the other
side ... where the work-card holders were taking their places ... I went on my own accord
to Becker because he had once told me that I
could remain with my family. There, I asked
him, if my wife and child can accompany me.
He said my wife can come with me to the
camp, but my child ('the shit' as he expressed
it) has to go. Of course we didn't want to separate from our child. I was forced to take my
place in the line of Jews who had been selected to work, while my wife remained with my
child and was apparently deported with the
others.[29]

Okay, enough.

When he testified in 1970, my father omitted some dramatic details from the story he gave in deposition four years earlier,
perhaps in a quixotic bid for credibility with this particular
judge. Or was this later telling easier to bear, more psycho-
logically palatable to my father, with its emphasis on his being
forced to separate from his wife and child and nothing about
force being exerted on her, i.e., her being clubbed over the head
and dragged away with their child? I don't know. Whatever, the
shit's name remains the same and the outcome doesn't change.

So, these are the facts. Each of my parents had had another
marriage, another spouse, another child that had met with a
brutal end in the war. My father's child (my half-brother) was
a boy, as Abe had thought. We later learned the boy was also
named Abraham, after my father's father, whose grave is in the

Jewish cemetery in Starachowice that the artist Frankiewicz tends. My mother's child, I don't know for sure but I would bet a girl (my half-sister). Luba had always wanted a girl, had seemed disappointed to give birth to boy after boy until the total of us brothers was five. She actually witnessed the murder of her first child! Is this what she sees on the screen of her hands when lighting the Shabbos candles? Her first husband, Rotvoegel, died of typhus, his body pissed on by a Nazi officer, an act of desecration that was witnessed by my father.

My father's deposition and testimony made no reference to his sisters, to his mother or grandparents, and that lack kept me wanting to read more. Luckily for me, Browning had included in his envelope statements from Uncle Srulec,[30] who also testified at Becker's trial, and Uncle Yankel, who was deposed but didn't testify. An unnamed sister of theirs, who was twelve at the time, Srulec tells us, was on her way to a bakery outside the ghetto without a permit when she was shot and killed. Their other two sisters and their mother (my grandmother), after being rounded up for the Selection at the marketplace, were shipped off by train to Treblinka and were never heard from again. Two uncles and a niece, says Srulec, were shot at the marketplace, and his eighty-year-old grandmother (my great-grandmother) was murdered in their house.

I'm devastated, bereft, having found these relatives going back three generations and lost them again. I will never know them. Nameless they shall remain.

The final document that Browning sent me was the deposition of Mina Binsztok. I am gobsmacked by its inclusion. I had not asked for it, didn't think of asking for it, and was unaware of her participation in these legal proceedings. Knowing nothing of her history, I read with great curiosity and no less trepidation.

Mina, like my mother, was born in Wierzbnik. Although she'd been a seamstress, her experience with Germans in Poland was not a result of her profession, as was my father's, but through her brother, a popular bootmaker. This is how she came to know many of the Nazis that were stationed in Starachowice. She saw much, remembered much, her descriptions of the main characters loaded with details perhaps only a seamstress or tailor would have noticed. She said one of the men, Baumgarten, wore a field gray uniform; another, Kaschmieder, usually sported knickerbockers; Schroth dressed in a light green, not a field grey, uniform. She describes *Lagerfuhrer* Althoff in the following way:

> He usually wore civilian clothes, dressed as follows: riding boots, ¾ jacket, hat with brim worked under on all sides and a submachine gun on a belt. I heard moreover that Althoff was a drug addict. He tormented people just to amuse himself.... One morning when we were finishing getting ready for work, I saw Althoff standing in the doorway to the men's section and shooting with his submachine gun.... We heard, in addition to the shooting, the screams, and I later saw countless dead outside the barracks who had tried to escape out the window. On the way to work in the vicinity of the barracks we walked literally in blood.[31]

Other figures of power Mina remembers by their descriptive nicknames. A fat, swarthy SS man they called "Tiger" — no smile ever crossed his lips. "Nasal" was another SS man. There was "Little Slant-eyes," and let's not forget "Butcher."

Mina's evidence, presumably like the testimony given by my father, Uncle Srulec, and other survivors, was not to be believed according to the presiding judge, simply because she was not a disinterested observer: "Before the evacuation, I saw the people hanging in the marketplace in Starachowice. I knew one of the dead, her maiden name was Luczkowitez, and her daughter, who was about 16 years old. These people had been in prison before this, had been members of the Polish Resistance. They were hanged on a Sunday, I remember clearly, because I saw the townspeople on their way to church. I was not present for the hanging of the Poles. But I remember seeing 16 dead...."[32]

Mina toiled in the Hermann Göring Munitions Works before the ghetto evacuation in 1942, then in the labour camps around Starachowice, the Strelnica and Majówka *lagers*. In 1944, her life took the same fateful route as Ralph and Luba's: "During the loading for Auschwitz, I only saw uniforms, can't remember any faces. I was packed into a locked cattle car with lots of people. We were all women. It was a clear, sunny day. Some people in our car, especially the children, died en route. We did not know where we were being transported to, learning only when we arrived that our destination was Auschwitz...."[33]

Mina had no relatives who survived the war: "In the night, while the escape attempt from the Majówka Lager was taking place — it was shortly before our deportation to Auschwitz — I heard shots. I was extremely anxious and crawled under the short structural supports of the barracks. The next morning I saw the dead, and among them my cousin, then about 20 years old, Hinda Binsztok."[34]

Mina never had visitors at Palmerston, at least none I was aware of. In her sworn statement, she specifically mentions, in addition to her cousin, her bootmaker brother, another brother named Ekiba, a sister, and Iszak, a brother-in-law, all of whom didn't make it. When I knew her, she was alone in the world, floating like a boat on water, buffeted by the tides. But not adrift, not unmoored. We Chaitons had become her anchor.

I am astonished by what I've just read and curiously close to elated that after so many years I have been able to find out biographical details of my mother, my father, and their families; of a half-brother and half-sister who were murdered; of my Uncles Srulec and Yankel, who were sent to Auschwitz, too; of my grandmother, great-grandmother, aunts, and great-uncles who were murdered; and, of Mina. My father, it turns out, was a man with a heart, someone who could feel, suffer, even be heroic, and this revelation shocked me almost more than anything I had learned. I had always thought of him as cowardly, dull, and ungenerous if unpredictable and prone to sudden outbursts of anger. And I was afraid of him.

Browning's book revealed that my father was brave, had even, according to his deposition, participated with Luba in an unsuccessful attempt to escape from the slave labour camp. He had been in close quarters with the enemy, watched, listened, probed in his own unobtrusive way. He saved the life of a man shot and left for dead, smuggled him into the barracks, got him medical attention and a job with a sympathetic SS man. Or was all this braggadocio, lies he had told himself, come to believe, wanted to believe, wanted others — like me — to believe? Yet he had not voluntarily divulged these incidents to me, stories that would have elicited my respect, despite having had ample opportunity to do so — and that is one reason I think they ring true. Another is that it explains the great respect my father received from members of his community, a reverence I never understood.

These revelations necessitated a radical shift in my thinking. I've come to think my father was not such a prick after all, was decent even, a mensch, someone I can be proud of. Of this I can be sure: he, like my mother, was a human being who had been twisted into and out of shape by unspeakably traumatic experiences. It was a history that shaped me and my brothers as well. It was a history that determined the course of our lives.

I now realized there was a direct connection between my roiling emotions when, as a teenager, I had tried to kill myself and what my father was going through at the time. It was 1967 and, recently deposed, he was about to return to Germany for the trial. This would be his first trip back since leaving the Belsen DP camp in the late forties. My father's safe existence in the "new country" was threatened, his present well-being challenged by a best-left-hidden past, one that he'd had no choice now but to unearth. I had no idea that this was so — as usual, nary a word had been spoken within my hearing — and I had no awareness that its emotional spillover was affecting me, with possible life-and-death consequences.

My father was also having his own experience with a psychiatrist at the same time that I was seeing one. He was being examined by a German psychiatrist hired by the Federal Republic of Germany to assess how much psychological damage had been done to Holocaust survivors under the Nazi regime in order to determine how much they should be compensated as reparations. I don't know what my father was asked, nor what he answered. I do remember his anger, though, when he was assessed as having just 10 percent damage.

"*Tsen protsent!*" he kept shouting. "*Tsen protsent!*"

I can recall the sound of my father's voice, the look of hurt and bewilderment in his eyes. At the time, I wondered if he was upset because his payout would be meager but I instinctively knew that wasn't the cause. He was angry because his suffering had been belittled. I remember feeling his pain, all the while not knowing what he had suffered. I was told later by my brother Charles that after receiving his psychiatric assessment, my father got into an argument with my mother and struck her.

I can't help wondering about agency and the interconnectedness of things, events, people. Maybe it was not my being insensitive to my parents that made me disappear. Maybe it was because I was hypersensitive to them. We draw to ourselves what we most fear, like iron to lodestone. Because, in that darkest period of their lives, they experienced the sudden loss of loved ones — indeed, each their own child! — that became their greatest fear. If it happened once, it could happen again. Though not openly discussed, it must have replayed so many times in their minds, worn a groove so deep in their psyche that its reverberation called the experience back to them. They knew it, had lived it, expected it could happen to them again at any time out of the blue. My disappearing was the iron to their lodestone, a magnet with a pull so powerful, I could not resist.

* * *

My parents appear in my dreams even today. In a dream, my father sits at a desk, teaching me how to decode various written symbols. I thought it odd, given that he was barely literate, certainly no scholar. Maybe it was just a wish I had carried over the years — if only it had been so. But my dream reveals

My mother, Luba, with my father, Rachmil, holding their first-born son, Abie, likely Bergen-Belsen DP camp, winter 1946–47.

it has been so. He is my mentor and has given me this gift — the writing of this book. The discovery of his story was the key that enabled me to decode my early life and the ghosts that inhibited my relationship with my parents, and for that, I am most grateful.

I shared with my brothers what I discovered about our parents' lives, including that they'd been slaves in their Polish town and that their *lager* experience was more Auschwitz than Bergen-Belsen, though I still don't know how they got from A to B-B. All were thankful for the revelations, but these were especially meaningful to Abe, who, having been born in the DP camp at Belsen, as had Charles, was now the only one in our nuclear family alive from that period.

17

Buttonholing the Past

ONE EVENING HARVEY, ABE, AND I HAD A MEET-ing at Abe's house with Howard Chandler, a vibrant and en-gaging friend of my parents, who lived in Wierzbnik and was only twelve when the war broke out. Mr. Chandler generously shared with us what he could. He told us that as a youngster, he was able to speak an un-Yiddish-accented Polish as a re-sult of having hung out, played, and fished with Polish friends, and this had helped him to survive. In the shtetl, he was good friends with my mother's only brother, who was younger than my mother and closer to Howard's age. Howard told us his name was Fulek. So Uncle Fulek was the dark-eyed young man whose picture was on my mother's dresser! And he disappeared one day early in the war and was never seen again, according to Howard, not because he'd gone out to get a newspaper, as my mother had told me, but because they needed fuel for heat. Fulek went to the railway station to search for coal that had fallen off passing freight trains, coal that was destined for munitions factories, and was shot. Uncle Srulec was arrested and sent to jail for a year for doing the same thing.

Howard was also transported to Auschwitz-Birkenau. He recalled the white arm band with the blue Star of David he had to wear. He spoke about some of my parents' Wierzbnik friends who were fellow prisoners. He mentioned Marty Baranek, who at one point was selected for the gas chamber by Dr. Mengele, but was able to save himself, thanks to his small stature, by crawling into a fireplace and hiding. Both Chandler and Baranek have been frequent tour guides to Poland and Auschwitz as part of the March of the Living.

Howard also talked about Birkenau, where half the camp, it seemed to him at the time, was German-speaking Roma, "*Tsigayner.*" One night, he heard engines running, dogs barking, and shots being fired. The next day there were no Roma left in the camp — all had disappeared. Hearing Mr. Chandler's first-person account was very moving, not least because of his openness and ease talking about his experiences. Harvey, Abe, and I felt chillingly close to our parents and what they had to go through to survive.

* * *

The documents I received from Christopher Browning arrived just as I was beginning to work with dramaturge Iris Turcott on a complete rewrite of my play. Some details and much of the flavour of my parents' stories found their way into the new script, which became in effect a new play, a four-character drama, *It Has to Go to the Finisher*. The first thing Iris asked me to do was not to write but to sew. Preferably on an industrial machine like the one my father had used. I told her I didn't know how to sew on a machine, that my father had refused to teach me.

"Doesn't matter. Just pick a scrap of material, maybe some wool suiting, sit at a machine — you have one at Big It Up, don't you? — and sew some straight lines. Just to get a feel for it."

I did, and it radically altered my corporeal sense of what my father did. Tailoring was to become deeply embedded in the new script.

Finding out the history of our parents allowed me to have a relationship with my brothers and has brought us all closer together. David says I'm a unifying force among the brothers, which, ironically, I also was when I was absent. When I needed funds to do a workshop of my play at Toronto's Factory Theatre, I appealed to my brothers for assistance. They generously donated the money to make this possible, each an equal amount, even covering Charles's share, as Charles was no longer with us. This was a touching and tremendous gift.

I now see my brothers and their families maybe once or twice a year, usually at a *simcha* or at a family Seder, held at Abe's, David's, or Harvey's house. Although everyone is very warm and loving with me, I can't help still feeling like somewhat of an alien. They all have grown children, and Abe and Harvey have grandchildren. I struggle sometimes at these large three-generation gatherings to remember all the names and exactly what their blood relationship is to me. Lindy, my partner, is very fond of everyone in the family and I joke about how they like her better than me. The female partners of the Chaiton boys get together frequently and, among other things, commiserate about the emotional failings of the Chaitons, what *Just Mercy* author and attorney Bryan Stevenson would call our "brokenness." The women feel a kind of closeness that the men are lacking.

I communicate with my brothers by email, usually about new details I've discovered in our family history. Abe's response is always laconic, sometimes maddeningly so, and often with a question or an additional detail I've overlooked or gotten wrong. Harvey's answers are more polite, if still brief, and invariably appreciative. David goes to town with verbose missives, erudite dissertations, replete with fractured Yiddish, that make me laugh, if not touch me deeply. My communication with David is intense but intermittent, occurring in binges of emails and phone conversations that continue over several days, then nothing for months. I never get together with Harvey or Abe for coffee or a meal or just to sit and chat and shoot the breeze. We never pick up the phone to call and say what's up. They don't call me if there's a family emergency. They rarely, if ever, ask me about my housemates and I don't know if it's because my chosen family is not on their radar or if they just feel uncomfortable talking about them. Harvey has never been to my house. Abe neither, except for that one time at Lisa's memorial when we lived north of the city. I can't blame them since I've only actually invited them once and that was to Lindy's condo, not to my communal home near High Park. With David, it's different.

In 2019, I invited David for a visit, his first to my home. It was New Year's Day — an auspicious time for new beginnings and a deeper dive into our reawakened relationship. He gave me a warm bear hug on entering. I asked if I could take his coat, which he removed and handed to me, a gorgeous dark navy topcoat. As soon as I felt its softness, I knew it was cashmere.

The coat was fully lined with lustrous silky satin. I looked at the label to see who had created this wonder.

"Oh, my God. It's B&R Custom Tailors!"

"Yeah, Dad made it for me."

"You're kidding! It looks brand new, but it's got to be what? Forty years old?"

"Forty-five.... It's funny, you know. I don't know what made me wear it today. I had lost track of the coat and Jessie [my niece, David's younger daughter] pulled it out of the back of a closet the other day and was admiring it. 'I wondered where that went,' I said to her. 'It's been years since I've worn it.'"

David was chatty and open with Terry and Paulene, the last members of my non-blood family. They welcomed him warmly. David, fascinated by the reality of their familial presence in my life, was full of questions. Topics of conversation ranged widely from the political to the philosophical and the personal. He felt at home, loved and respected.

David brought me a present, a photo I'd never seen of my father (who, with hair on his head, looked in his thirties) sitting comfortably on a horse! You mean he actually could ride? Maybe he wasn't lying about being a Cossack after all. David said Dad, in his later years, used to brag about how popular he'd been in eastern Europe. Riding into various towns, he said he was always greeted by throngs of children shouting, "*Tateh, tateh!*" as if he had fathered them all — so typical of his over-the-top boasting and mischievous sense of humour.

I'd been studying Yiddish and we spoke it together, David and I, making up words to fill in the blanks in our memories, and we laughed. I shared with him the pleasure my classes have given me, getting to replay in my mind what the voices of our parents sounded like in their original tongues, and the sadness that they were no longer around to converse with.

"Sadness," David said, "is a legacy of our upbringing. It travels with us always."

* * *

My research into family history continues. I was aware that my Auntie Sallah's testimony had been memorialized on tape for the USC Shoah Foundation project initiated by Steven Spielberg. She was interviewed in 1997 for its Visual History Archive. After years of putting it off, I asked myself, "why?" Was I avoiding the horror, the helplessness, the not wanting to have to alter the image I carried of my cherished aunt? I finally made my way to the Neuberger Holocaust Education Centre in North York to view the digital archive.[35]

Sallah blew me away. Her mind at the time of taping was sharp; her memory of names, dates, places, unhesitating; her English vocabulary flawless. I was captivated by the description of her childhood in Poland, her fourteen aunts and uncles, all of whom she could name, her love of reading and books, her inability to continue to high school ("Gymnasium") because of a lack of money. And then what happened to her when she was fifteen and the war broke out.

Three moments in her testimony moved me to tears. Maybe because this was where my aunt cried the hardest. One was when she learned early in the war that her parents, brothers, and a sister had perished — that she and one sister, Henka, were left alone in the world. The second was on a transport train to Ravensbruck, the brutal concentration camp for women. Corpses lined the floor of the cattle car she'd been crammed into. She thought to herself, "Well at least we don't have to sit on the bare floor." She had grown hard, come to trust no one, her shaved head mute testimony to the bleakness of her outlook. It filled her with despair to see and listen to people suffer: "They couldn't even die!" Any seeming break she thought was a trick. Even when liberated, having crossed the border into Denmark and provided with food and a cot, she was still wary and disbelieving. Two months later, she was shipped to Sweden. And so began the third episode of tears. Speaking about the Swedish people she'd met, she cried remembering how incredibly kind they were to her: "They treated me like I was a human being."

As much as I had imagined her suffering, nothing equalled seeing and hearing my aunt, her familiar face that I dearly loved, talk about her youthful life and the unspeakable things she endured. With memories so mercilessly frozen in time that, even at age seventy-three, her expression was that of an uncomprehending teenage girl.

After a long bout with Alzheimer's, Auntie Sallah died in March 2023, her life a year short of a century. At her funeral, cousin Alf enlisted me to serve as a pallbearer and I was honoured. I wanted to bear her weight. After her simple casket was lowered into the ground, I joined the family in shovelling earth upon it. This mitzvah, an age-old tradition to help the deceased leave this vale, connected me to my history and sent my heart soaring. Sallah Chaiton was the last of her generation. Her husband Yankel, Auntie Basha and Uncle Srulec, and Ralph and Luba, my parents, all long departed, all buried in that same Wierzbniker section of the cemetery. May their memories be a blessing.

For the first time, I felt a need to view my parents' graves. Snow had freshly fallen over the field, and my footprints revealed the path I took to where my mother and father were buried side by side. Upon their joint headstone, I placed a pebble I had found long ago and kept with me as a treasured amulet. Dark and cool, it fit neatly in the palm of my hand, smooth to the touch except for where it was etched with the fossilized figures that had been my muses.

* * *

I was determined to investigate how my parents got accepted for immigration to Canada, how they were able to purchase the house on Palmerston on the meagre income of a tailor, and anything else I could find about my parents' lives. There was a time in the twentieth century when Jews were not permitted to emigrate to Canada. As Irving Abella and Harold Troper detailed in *None Is Too Many*, their now-classic history of Canada and the Jews of Europe, the prospect of Jewish immigration was considered anathema for most of the thirties, during the Second World War, and even just after, when the horrors of the Nazi death camps had been widely revealed. From 1933–1945, only five thousand Jewish refugees were accepted, "a record that is arguably the worst of all possible refugee-receiving states."[36] To circumvent the prohibition, the Canadian Jewish Congress along with a group of garment manufacturers, needle trade unions, and the Jewish Labour Committee, collaborated on a brilliant idea to make it possible for Jewish refugees to gain entry into the country; namely, to fill a putative shortage of workers in the needle trades. Their lobbying of the federal government was successful, and the admission for two thousand craftsmen for the clothing industry was approved. Originally called the Overseas Garment Workers Scheme, it is known today as the Tailor Project.

All was not smooth sailing, however. The moment Mackenzie King's government realized that most of the tailors in the scheme would be Jewish, the number of any one racial group was summarily limited to half of the total. C.D. Howe, the minister of reconstruction and supply, informed one of the creators of the scheme, Max Enkin, of this eleventh-hour change to what was supposed to have been an unrestricted process. Already in Europe as part of the Overseas Garment Workers Selection Team, Enkin was stunned when, as he recalled years later, Howe told him categorically that "under no circumstances would the government proceed if more than fifty percent of the total were Jews."[37] Nevertheless, after sufficient numbers of non-Jewish garment workers could not be found, the quota was upped slightly by a reluctant minister of immigration. Eventually, about 2,500 tailors were accepted into Canada under the program, 60 percent of them, Jews.[38]

Program participants were required to commit to labouring in a garment factory for one year while repaying the cost of train transport from Halifax to Montreal, Toronto, Winnipeg, Vancouver, or wherever they were contracted. You didn't actually need to be a tailor to qualify but you needed to be able to sew a buttonhole. A number of people in the DP camps located in Germany and Austria were taught this task so they could finally leave and build a new life in Canada. My father was one of their teachers.

Despite the government's preference for smaller families with no more than one child, which was to keep the overall number of Jewish immigrants as low as possible, my father, with my mother, Luba, and my two older brothers, documented as Abram and Chil, made the grade. My father's exceptional tailoring skills likely accounted for this allowance. As I discovered from research at

Canadian Garment Workers Selected in British Zone of Germany. P 1
October 12th., 1947

NICHOLS

No	Name	Sex.	M.S.	Child.	Pers.	Nat'l	Age	City
1	Gudziunas	M	M	1	R.C.	Lith	55	
5	Naginonis	M	S	0	R.C.	Lith	50	
6	Chapla	M	M	0	G.C.	Pol.U.	45	
7	Gadinovitch	M	M	0	G.C.	Pol.U.	46	
8	Novosad	M	M	1	G.C.	Pol.	33	
10	Kovalenko	M	S	0	G.C.	Pol	53	
11	Kuzneciv	F	S	0	G.C.	Pol	38	
15	Plasecka	F	S	0	R.C.	Pol	45	
17	Gerlach	M	M	1	R.C.	Pol	39	
18	Zacharko	M	S	0	G.C.	Ukr.	24	W
19	Koluss	M	M	1	R.C.	Lat.	38	
22	Shuper	M	M	2	G.C.	Pol.U.	22	
23	Tynczuk	M	M	1	G.C.	Pol.U.	25	
25	Dendura	M	M	0	G.C.	Pol.U.	28	
26	Teplyj	M	M	0	G.C.	Pol.U.	27	T
27	Sakowsky	M	S	0	G.C.	Pol.U.	24	
28	Stefaniuk	M	S	0	G.C.	Pol.U	40	
29	Lisnyj	M	S	0	G.C.	Pol.U	25	
30	Hostiuk	M	S	0	G.C.	Pol.U	24	
32	Witiuk	M	S	0	G.C.		32	
33	Diskowski	M	M	0	R.C.		33	T
34	Wilk	M	M	1	R.C.		27	
51	Sveikauskas	M	M	2	R.C.		34	
55	Kvetkauskas	M	S	0	R.C.		46	
60	Zaskevisius	M	S	0	R.C.		34	
61	Abramowies	M	M	1	Jewish		22	
62	Awronski	M	M	0	Jewish		37	
63	Binsztok Mina	F	S	0	Jewish		31	T
64	Bialik	M	M	1	Jewish		33	T
65	Baumel	M	M	0	Jewish		32	W
66	Buchvalter	M	M	1	Jewish		27	
67	Chaiton Dacimil	M	M	1	Jewish		32	T

List of Canadian Garment Workers Selected in British Zone of Germany, October 12, 1947. My father is 67th on the list; Mina, is 63rd. (Ontario Jewish Archives, F70_f3_i002.)

the Ontario Jewish Archives, the four of them arrived in Canada at Halifax's Pier 21 on October 1, 1948, having sailed on the *General W.C. Langfitt*, the only Jewish family on board with two children. On the same ship, according to the ship's manifest, was a single female with no children — Mina Binsztock!

After arriving in Toronto on October 4, my family stayed for a short time in Council House at 44 St. George Street, the home of the National Council of Jewish Women of Canada. A wide array of Jewish organizations and social service agencies were mobilized to smooth the transition for the new immigrants, providing housing, furniture, transportation, translation, English language classes, and more. They moved to 591 Palmerston Avenue where they rented the living room, for which Rachmil's monthly pay was garnished thirty dollars. Four other survivor families also rented rooms in the house at the same time. Within a year, Rachmil was able to purchase the Canadian Jewish Congress–owned house thanks to two mortgages and a loan of $1,500 from a family member. I'm guessing this was Avrum Bleeman, my mother's cousin who was to become my godfather.

One of Rachmil's first jobs was at Belmont Cloak at 96 Spadina Avenue. The factory was located in the garment district just one block from 58 Spadina Avenue, the future headquarters for Big It Up Hats, where I went to work some fifty years later, perhaps feeling the magnetic pull of place and energy without knowing why.

Another curiosity surfaced in my research. My father told us his birthday was April 15, and indeed that date was when our "Happy Birthday, *Tateh*" greetings were forthcoming. I took it for granted that he was an Aries — the polar opposite of me, a Libra. A photograph in the Ontario Jewish Archives of a billboard at Bergen-Belsen made me question this. It shows that the concentration camp was liberated by the British in 1945 on the 15th of April. An unbelievable cosmic coincidence? Or did Rachmil adopt that date as his birthday? Why not? It marked the first day of his emergence into the light, of his birth into a new life. A document I recently found in Germany's Arolsen Archive lists his birthday as February 22 — a Pisces. Who knows? So much was hidden and unspoken, so much still to be discovered and uncovered.

In 2019, an event to commemorate Tailor Project families and their contribution to Canada was held at Toronto's Holy Blossom Synagogue. Called "A Common Thread," it was attended by over 1,200 people, including Prime Minister Justin Trudeau, who gave an inspirational speech. In 2020, *The Tailor Project* was published by Second Story Press, whose publisher is Margie Wolfe. I went to junior high school with Margie. Her parents were, like mine, both survivors from Wierzbnik; and Margie, like my older brothers, was born in the Belsen DP camp. In a recent phone conversation, she told me that my mother and her mother played poker together in the Tikvah Club. Margie fondly recalls when, as a girl, she would sit at her kitchen table with her mother and mine and try on various lipsticks. My mother at the time was an Avon lady.

I've since returned to the Ontario Jewish Archives to search for records of the five-man delegation who scouted the DP camps in Germany and Austria in 1947. Among the files of Samuel Posluns, who was on the team as a representative of the Cloak Manufacturers Association of Toronto, I found two items that made me tremble.

One was an airmail envelope from N. Kirsh of 337 Brunswick Avenue addressed to Rachmil Chajton at the Belsen DP camp, postmarked Toronto, July 17, 1947, a month before the selection

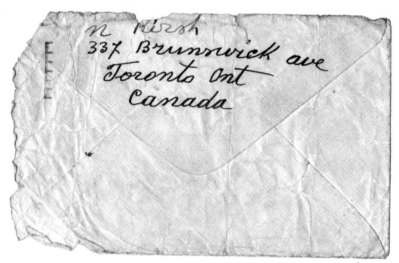

This and following page: Envelope and letter, handwritten in Yiddish, to my mother from N. Kirsh; mailed from Toronto to my father in Belsen DP camp, July 17, 1947. (Ontario Jewish Archives, F70_f9_i002.)

Toronto July 17 - 47.

Members of the Overseas Garment Workers Commission selection team, likely at Bergen-Belsen DP camp, with officials and displaced persons, 1947. The partially obscured face peering out at the centre rear could be my father. (Ontario Jewish Archives, F70_f3_i002.)

team were to arrive in Europe. Unlike all the other envelopes in the file, which were empty, this one had a letter inside.

Handwritten in blue-inked Yiddish, it begins, "Dear Lubeleh," then goes on to inform my mother that my father's name has been registered with the Canadian Jewish Congress and to please "save yourselves" by meeting with the people who are visiting the camps, looking for tailors to bring over to Canada to fill a labour shortage. The letter ends with, "Remain well. With heartfelt greetings from my husband and all the children, from me, your Auntie, who hopes to see you all."

I wept reading it, knowing that this fragile piece of paper, so full of hope for the future, was touched by the hands of my mother and my father. The letter's presence in these files is both a mystery and a gift.

The other item is a small black-and-white photographic slide, about two inches square. It's a group shot of selected garment workers, men and women from the Belsen camp, standing in a semi-circle with the Canadian delegation outside a nondescript brick building. My eyes are drawn to the centre of the back row, to a partially obscured face breaking into a wry smile. It's a face that, at age thirty-two, looks uncannily like me.

I'm going to share it with my brothers.

Epilogue

MUCH THAT I LEARNED WORKING ON RUBIN'S case enabled me to finally discover my parents' stories. Patience, persistence, perseverance, fearlessness — these qualities, along with my skills in research, were honed while helping Rubin Carter regain his freedom. They similarly helped to liberate my mother and father, to bring their stories from captivity in the dark night of the untold and unremembered into the shining freedom of the never-to-be-forgotten.

That the trajectory of my parents' lives was scarily similar to Rubin's is clearer to me in retrospect. The unjustness of their incarceration based entirely on racism rather than reason. The bitter truth that, in some respects, their sentences, like Rubin's, began the day they got out of prison. "When will it be good?" my father would ask. None of them could bring themselves to look back with intention, to be open about and tackle head on their nightmarish imprisonment and the psychological scars it produced. They seemed never to be happy, my parents; neither did Rubin. Despite it all, like Rubin, they were able to carve out a significant life for themselves post-incarceration. My brothers tell me that life was better for my father and mother as they aged. And they had *naches* from their sons who were successful professionals and from their grandchildren, on whom, I'm told, they doted.

While writing, I was never sure I'd show this manuscript to any of my brothers. I was apprehensive they would disapprove of my portrayal of them or my inclusion of intimate details of their lives they'd prefer to keep to themselves. I was afraid resurrecting long-buried issues might trigger and anger them, so I decided to follow my parents' code and say nothing. But I've come to realize this work is, in part, an apologia to my brothers, an explication of my behaviour toward them and the family, not that they ever demanded one. It is also a document that bears witness to all of our lives, including that of my parents, and thus concerns them profoundly. Keeping silent has led to separation in our lives; sharing this narrative could pull us all closer. Yes, it's better to know. So, I changed my mind.

Once I had a completed manuscript draft, I called David to arrange to meet in person. I went to his house and we had coffee. I talked at length about the memoir, how it came about, what the writing process was like. I brought a hard copy with me but hadn't yet decided whether I'd let him see it. I needed to see how he reacted to my introduction to the project. He was wholeheartedly attentive and enthusiastic, and expressed great interest in reading it. I didn't think it would be a mistake to give it to him. Indeed, I would cherish his insight and input.

At a Hannukah brunch at Harvey's, I mentioned the memoir to Harvey and Abe, who both eagerly said they'd love to read it. I sent each of them an electronic copy. I encouraged all my brothers to send me their thoughts, even as they were reading.

Scarcely two hours had gone by before I heard back from Abe, and Harvey and David followed soon after with a barrage of missives. They were moved by my honesty and the plethora of details I recalled, most of which they'd forgotten, had never known, or hadn't understood in context. They relished the opportunity and perspective that hindsight afforded, so much so that they each opened up to me in a way they hadn't done before, almost as a confessional.

Abe recalled that he, too, realized early on that my mother had trouble accepting gifts, so after a point, wouldn't even try to give her anything. He also recognized that he'd had a hard time asking for what he wanted, that he was not attuned to his own needs. He said we brothers "didn't really know who we were, or who we needed as partners." He, Charlie, and David, who ended up divorcing their first wives shortly after our parents died, "chose who we thought they liked." The manuscript prompted other insights. Abe said he now understood "Dad's boasting ... was just mimicking what he overheard from the German soldiers when he was a servant to Becker."

My story inspired Abe to share his own stories, and I was deeply stirred. He told me about a woman who had come to his office for treatment one day many years ago. She had known our parents and was in the marketplace in Wierzbnik at the time of the Roundup in October 1943: "She said she could still see dad's [first] wife and son all dressed up along with the grandmother marching toward the centre of the town under duress." Abe couldn't recall who the patient was, but the encounter shook him up.

Harvey said reading the manuscript helped him to better understand me and our parents. I think it also gave him insight into himself: "I witnessed the challenges mom and dad had ... and I chose not to make waves. I was the 'good boy.' I have dad's work ethic and locked-up emotion."

David commented that he thought he'd known me well, "like an old intimate chum," but the reading revealed his "nescience." His lapping up the manuscript was bittersweet for him because "a wound has been opened that can never quite heal": "Those years are gone. Storytelling is postprandial by its very nature and while satisfying in so many ways, is not the same as enjoying the meal together."

David went on to say that the book taught him many things he's only beginning to realize. Over the years, he struggled with and questioned his own depression, fear, and anhedonia, thinking, "I wasn't in the war, or the camps. I didn't lose anyone I knew or cared for. I have lived a life of privilege. Why do I feel this way?" David wondered whether "our parents and our brothers were/are victims and survivors in equal measure."

The research, writing, and sharing of this story have amounted to a kind of healing for me and my brothers, offering us all a look into ourselves and our histories, and fostering a feeling of closeness and, indeed, fraternal love we had until now been unable to express. What would my parents have thought about my reunion with my brothers and the new relationships we have forged? Certainly, they would have regretted not being around to be part of it. And they would have been gratified that the family was able to surmount separation, disappearance, disappointment, loss.

For me, survival depended on disappearing in the same way my mother's and father's survival depended on their silence. Maybe not the best course of action for any of us, but could we have done things differently? I wish my parents were here so I could ask them, preferably in the language of their youth. Our relationship might be able to proceed on an entirely different footing, with talk, forgiveness, and mutual appreciation free-flowing. Tonight I shall dream them alive.

Acknowledgements

THIS MEMOIR OWES ITS LIFE TO THE LOVE AND care of a wide circle of support, inspiration, encouragement, and contribution. To the generous and kind individuals who helped make this book a reality, I offer this thanksgiving.

My deepest gratitude goes to my love and partner, Lindy Green, who provided a critical knock at the door of my late parents' untold history that I thought had been forever closed to my brothers and me. Lindy was the first to encourage me to write a memoir. She read countless drafts over the years, always with new eyes, fresh interest, and an unfailing belief in the value of the story and my ability to do it justice, despite persistent self-doubt.

A huge thank you to Holocaust historian Christopher R. Browning, whose devastating book, *Remembering Survival:*

Inside a Nazi Slave-Labor Camp, unlocked that door and sparked my need to open it further. When I contacted Dr. Browning for more information specific to my family, he generously sent me copies of documents from his research of the German war crimes trial of Walther Becker, against whom my father had testified.

To the formidable Rubin "Hurricane" Carter, whose 2014 Easter Sunday death prompted me to review the role I played in Rubin's life and to see his incarceration and liberation in the context of that of my parents'.

To Lesra Martin for indulging my recounting of some of his early life. I thank him for staying in tune with and true to his loving and loveable, curious younger self.

Profound thanks to the late dramaturge and editor Iris Turcott, who was convinced of the book-worthiness of my life's drama. Iris challenged me to let it flow without judgment. Knowing her red pen was poised to slash with panache made it paradoxically easier to bare myself. Iris left us early in this process but without her midwifery, this book would never have been born.

With abounding gratitude to my brothers Abe, David, and Harvey for their acceptance of my wayward ways, their thoughts about and corrections to the manuscript, and their magnanimity in allowing me to use their words and sensitive autobiographical details. And to my late brother Charles, who will always be Charlie to me.

For also helping me discover family history and revelatory archival materials: cousins Alf Chaiton and Gail Buxbaum, aunt Sallah Chaiton, sister-in-law Karen Chaiton, and Howard Chandler. Thank you to Janice Rosen (Canadian Jewish Archives), Donna Bernardo-Ceriz (Ontario Jewish Archives),

Neuberger Holocaust Education Centre, Margie Wolfe, and Paula Draper (*The Tailor Project*) for their generous assistance.

In deep appreciation of their support and expert substantive editorial ideas — or suggestions on where to find them: Jim Polk, Iris Tupholme, Scott Sellers, Cynthia Good, Barbara Berson, Wendy Atkinson.

For conversations providing perspective, insight, and impetus, special thanks to Pearl Goodman, Nicolas Billon, Denise Fujiwara, Weyni Mengesha, and Alan Dilworth. And for providing a conducive writing space and encouraging me to keep submitting my manuscript to publishers: Andrea Weissman-Daniels and Mark Daniels. For a listening ear and reading eye: Karen and Donna Green, Susan Macpherson, Patricia Fraser, Flavio Belli, Joanne McLean, and Arthur Lockhart. For teaching me Yiddish with enthusiasm and delight and for invaluable assistance with translation, thank you to Sharon Power. To George Fischer for help with translation into Hungarian and to Johanna Bergfeldt for similar assistance with Swedish. Thank you to Ed Roth for my author photo and his work on restoring archival photographs.

With gratitude to John Eagle Shield for introducing me to Indigenous history and culture, to Vern Harper for continuing these teachings, and *kinanâskomitin* to Paulene Shirt and Clayton Shirt for welcoming our group into their Cree family.

To my intentional family members, Kathy Swinton and Paulene Harvey, profound gratitude for reading early drafts and adding their weight to this book. How blessed was I to have been able to share the major part of my life with them. I miss them both, their laughter and uncompromisingly serious approach to living. To Terry Swinton, my intellectual co-conspirator, whom I can't thank enough for our deep bond. I love the serendipity and sympatico-ness of our writing together, first on the federal court briefs for Rubin Carter, then his post-release speeches, then *Lazarus and the Hurricane*, and then our collaboration on the movie *The Hurricane*, working with Armyan Bernstein and Rudy Langlais on the screenplay. Thank you to Terry, too, for permission to use material from *Lazarus and the Hurricane* herein. On this book as well, Terry has diligently read and reread manuscript sections, sharing insights and suggestions with love and ferocity. Rest in peace, my brother.

To Paula David, Ezra Dubrow, Bev Spring, and Stephen Cole, for championing this book. Paula helped me see my work in a new light and canvassed colleagues Arielle Berger and others, for suggestions on next steps. To Aefa Mulholland, who provided an invaluable list, which spurred me on to find not only a publisher, but also an agent. To Julia Kim, my editor, my eternal gratitude. Her immediate and unreserved enthusiasm, sensitivity, openness, and insightful editing skills made a welcoming home for my memoir. With thanks for their consummate professionalism to Kwame Scott Fraser, Meghan Macdonald, Chris Houston, Laura Boyle, Erin Pinksen, and all the good folks at Dundurn Press. Thanks also to copy editor Carrie Gleason for her fact-checking and staunch advocacy for the reader. Also in my corner, I'm thrilled to have as my agent the brilliant Kathryn Willms and Sam Hiyate of The Rights Factory.

And to my parents, Ralph and Luba Chaiton, to whom this memoir is dedicated. May it bring them the *naches* I was unable to when they were alive.

Notes

1   Wikipedia, s.v. "High Park Forest School," last modified March 26, 2021, 17:43 (UTC), en.wikipedia.org/wiki /High_Park_Forest_School#cite_note-7.

2   Shout out to Michael Wex's "Old Farts Watching Wrestling" in *Born to Kvetch* (New York: Harper Perennial, 2006), 6.

3   Wex, 6.

4   Selwyn Raab, "Artis and Carter, in Different Prison Atmospheres, Seek Another Trial," *New York Times*, December 18, 1977, nytimes.com/1977/12/18/archives/artis-and-carter -in-different-prison-atmospheres-seek-another-trial.html.

5   Vincent DeSimone, Acting Chief of Passaic County Detectives, Grand Jury Testimony, Paterson, New Jersey, June 1966, Rubin "Hurricane" Carter collection, F0786, York University Libraries, Toronto.

6   Carter v. Dietz, 621 F.Supp. 533,559 (D.N.J. 1985).

7   Carter v. Dietz, 621 F.Supp. 533,559 (D.N.J. 1985).

8   Transcript of Nov 8, 1985 Enlargement Proceedings, FDCNJ, Rubin "Hurricane" Carter collection, F0786, York University Libraries, Toronto.

9   Selwyn Raab, "Witnesses in Jersey Triple Murder Recant Testimony 7 Years After 2 Got Life," *New York Times*, September 27, 1974, 56.

10   Ralph V. Martin, J.S.C., Superior Court of New Jersey Passaic County, Order for Dismissal of Indictment No. 167-66, February 26, 1988, Paterson, New Jersey.

11   Logan Jenkins, "Judge Who Freed Hurricane Mourns Death of Friend," *San Diego Union-Tribune*, April 22, 2014, sandiegouniontribune.com/lifestyle/people/sdut-judge-free -hurricane-mourns-friend-2014apr22-story.html.

12   Kent Roach, *Wrongfully Convicted: Guilty Pleas, Imagined Crimes, and What Canada Must Do to Safeguard Justice*, (Toronto: Simon & Schuster, 2023), xxxi.

13   Over the years, I have been fortunate to work on various readings and workshops of this play with outstanding actors and directors, lauded veterans like Don Francks ("Iron Buffalo"), Paul Soles, Richard McMillan, and Theresa Tova; the incomparable Rwandan Canadian musician/composer/singer The Mighty Popo (Jacques Murigande, Che's cousin); and with rising stars like Andre Sills, Cara Ricketts, and director Weyni Mengesha. Working with the actor Alon Nashman as a director, we developed the piece into a play with music entitled *Noah's Great Rainbow*, a phrase I lifted from Bob Dylan's "Desolation Row." Music was by the multi-talented musicians and composers Waleed Abdulhamid, David Buchbinder, and Popo Murigande; lyrics were written by Alon, Don Francks, and me. The Black/white, Muslim/Jewish/Christian/pagan collaboration by its very nature told the story I wanted to tell.

14   Christopher R. Browning, *Remembering Survival: Inside a Nazi Slave-Labor Camp* (New York: W.W. Norton, 2010), 1.

15   Browning, 2.

16   Browning, 2.

17   Browning, 2.

18   Browning, 47.

19   Browning, 47.

20   Browning, 31n46.

21   Browning, 97–98.

22 Ralph Chaiton, Deposition, Toronto, Canada, 28 September 1966, in the Investigation against Becker and others for national-socialistic violent crime in … Starachowice … 1940–1944, File Number 141 Js 1312/63, the Directing Chief District Attorney, District Court of Hamburg, p.3.

23 Chaiton, 3–4.

24 Chaiton, 5.

25 Chaiton, 5.

26 Chaiton, 6–7.

27 Chaiton, 7.

28 Ralph Chaiton, Testimony, 2 November 1970, in the Preliminary Investigation of Walther Becker for Murder, Hamburg District Court fil 556/8/67, Hamburg, p. 5.

29 Ralph Chaiton, Testimony, 2 November 1970, in the Preliminary Investigation of Walther Becker for Murder, Hamburg District Court fil 556/8/67, Hamburg, p. 5.

30 Israel Chaiton, Deposition, Toronto, Canada, 14 March 1967, in the Investigation against Becker and others for national-socialistic violent crime in … Starachowice … 1940–1944, File Number 141 Js 1312/63, the Directing Chief District Attorney, District Court of Hamburg, 2–4.

31 Mina Binsztok, Deposition, Toronto, Canada, 16 December 1966, in the Investigation against Becker and others for national-socialistic violent crime in … Starachowice … 1940–1944, File Number 141 Js 1312/63, the Directing Chief District Attorney, District Court of Hamburg, 4.

32 Binsztok, 3.

33 Binsztok, 5–6.

34 Binsztok, 7.

35 Sara Chaiton, Video Interview, USC Shoah Foundation, Interview Code 32741, August 14, 1997.

36 Irving Abella and Harold Troper, *None Is Too Many: Canada and the Jews of Europe*, (Toronto: University of Toronto Press, 1983, 2000, 2012), xx.

37 Max Enkin, Oral History Interview, April 1986, Larry Enkin Collection, Ontario Jewish Archives, Toronto.

38 Author's February 3, 2020, telephone conversation with Paula Draper, co-author of *The Tailor Project: How 2,500 Holocaust Survivors Found a New Life in Canada* (Toronto: Second Story Press, 2020).

About the Author

SAM CHAITON is a Toronto author and playwright, a dancer, entrepreneur, and long-time social justice advocate. His first book, co-authored with Terry Swinton, was the international non-fiction bestseller *Lazarus and the Hurricane*, which became a basis for the Norman Jewison film *The Hurricane* starring Denzel Washington. In the movie, Liev Schreiber portrays Sam, one of "the Canadians" who helped unjustly imprisoned Rubin Carter regain his freedom.

Sam and Terry have recently donated 4.9 metres of textual records, including their investigative notes and legal research in the Carter case (1966–1988), to create the Rubin "Hurricane" Carter collection at York University Libraries.

Sam lives with his partner, Lindy Green, in Toronto, where they are ardent supporters of the performing and visual arts; equity and access in health care and research; and Innocence Canada (formerly the Association in Defence of the Wrongly Convicted), which Sam helped found.

A fitness buff, Sam still takes contemporary dance classes. He also loves baking vegan desserts.